SEE
HOW
THE
WIND
BLOWS

SEE HOW THE WIND BLOWS

by **Bob Slosser**

*The Holy Spirit
Nudges the Church Toward Unity*

*Logos International
Plainfield, New Jersey*

All Scripture, unless otherwise noted, is taken from the New International Version. Italics have been added by the author for emphasis.

To
Harald Bredesen,
Terry Fullam
and Pat Robertson

Contents

Preface

It is a truism that to understand where we're going, we should frequently look back at where we've been. God kept reminding the people of Israel of that as he led them toward the Promised Land. The advice is certainly true for the people of God today. We have been in the midst of one of the strongest religious revivals in history, and as we wonder at its future, we would do well to examine, if only briefly, what we have learned from its past.

This book attempts to do that—to provide a quick overview of this current movement of God that is usually referred to as the charismatic renewal and to peer into the mist toward its fulfillment.

Two truths stand out clearly:

1. The Holy Spirit is a missionary Spirit.
2. The Holy Spirit is a Spirit of unity.

SEE HOW THE WIND BLOWS

CHAPTER ONE

A Quieter Breeze

It was right after Pentecost Sunday, 1978. I couldn't get over what had happened here in New Jersey, up near the Lincoln Tunnel into New York. If the estimates were anywhere near accurate, 55,000 Christians of just about every stripe possible—Catholics and Protestants of all sorts—had joined together that Saturday before Pentecost in Giants Stadium in the Meadowlands to speak, shout, and sing praises to Jesus Christ. It had been one of America's most unusual Christian witnesses.*

As I reflected on the beauty of the unity shining in that vast wasteland for six hours on a cloudy, spring Saturday, my mind drifted back to my first real taste of such ecumenism eleven years earlier. It was unity on a much different scale, a time when rallies and conferences of thirty, forty, and fifty thousand people—Catholics or Protestants—were undreamed of. It was a time of a quieter breeze.

*   *   *   *

My watch showed 8:30. It was a hot, humid Monday

_____

*A year later similar rallies across the country were attended by more than 200,000 people.

1

morning in the nervous city of Mount Vernon, New York, a hotbed of racial strife in the violence that shook America that year, 1967. In a quiet basement room of the First Reformed Church's school building, eleven widely dissimilar people prayed as a new day unfolded in one of Christianity's significant modern periods. I was one of the eleven.

The youngest that morning was fourteen—crew cut, slender, quick; the oldest was forty-nine—baldish, chubby, not so quick, but eager. All sat on the floor. There were no chairs, only a mat rug. On one lightly painted wall hung a cross made from tree branches and still bearing the bark. Its arms were angled upward—"for the ascension," I was told. The trunk and arms both still had leaves and traces of buds—"life." On a table in front of the cross were two oversized candles and a large, open Bible. Everything was simple.

Three of the eleven were Roman Catholics, two were Pentecostals, and the rest were from the so-called mainline Protestant establishment: Methodist, Baptist, Congregational, Reformed. Absent that morning because of part-time jobs were three other young Catholics and an older Protestant.

I leaned against one wall and watched and listened to the ten others, all gathered at the church of the oldest member, Harald Bredesen, with the purpose of reaching Mount Vernon for Christ. I knew only a few of them. Watching and listening, I couldn't tell them apart, Protestant from Catholic, Pentecostal from Baptist. Wide-eyed and eager, they read from the Bible, they spoke to God, they listened for God to speak to them, they forthrightly and simply asked God to touch the people of that city. Sometimes they wept.

That Monday morning, the beginning of their third week there, they talked about their encounters with unbelievers. There was laughter, but there was exasperation too, even some momentary anger.

A young married woman, a recent graduate of Duquesne University in Pittsburgh, brushed her long brown hair away from her eyes, but it fell back. She repeated the motion every now and then as she wrestled verbally with the fears they were arousing among a lot of the young people they were meeting who had some sort of Catholic background.

"You can't understand how afraid they are." She looked quickly at a young member of Bredesen's church, then at Harald, and then at a young man next to her. Her bright eyes seemed to flatten in dismay.

"But I can tell you from my own experience that they are terrified when brought close to something so alien, so Protestant"—she couldn't suppress a smile—"so far from what they've grown up with. They feel threatened."

She shrugged and looked at the floor. "I know I was terrified when I found myself moving away from the calm, quiet, protected tradition I'd grown up in and started moving toward some sort of association with Protestants. It wasn't till Ralph finally got across to us that we had to stop trying to live for the Catholic church, or the Protestant church, or any such thing, and to live for Christ—it was then that the fear of losing all our security began to go away. But it was real fear up to then." The "Ralph" was Ralph Martin, now a prominent lay leader in the Catholic charismatic renewal.

Another young woman echoed the theme, but from the Protestant view. "I was afraid all my freedom and all my integrity were going to be corrupted," she said. She didn't smile.

The Lord, beginning about five months earlier, had taken those very different people through many delicate, sometimes shattering, moments to get them to the fragile state of unity they were living through that morning. That unity was the fruit of the Holy Spirit. Because of him—the wind of the Lord—and only because of him were they there in that strange place that morning. They had opened their hearts wide to Christ; he was their Lord and Savior, very specifically. And quite naturally, it seemed, they had found their hearts opened wide to one another.

But their encounter with Jesus had not stopped there. They had been baptized in the Holy Spirit, according to the promises of Scripture. And each had experienced manifestations of that baptism, speaking and praying in tongues, prophesying, praying effectually for the sick. They had received power in their unity.

The drawing together of the group—originally twenty but averaging fifteen or sixteen throughout most of the summer as some went on jobs and other ministries—appeared to have begun on the Duquesne campus the previous winter. Working reportedly through two or three members of the faculty, God had poured out his Spirit there in an awesome way.

He revealed his power in numerous instances, one of the most striking times coming early in the experience at a weekend retreat devoted to consideration of the Acts of the Apostles. Unexpectedly, the well went dry at the retreat center, a fact confirmed by a man called to check the pump. A few agreed it was time to stop talking about the power of God and to call upon it. They said that if the retreat was in the will of God, as they believed, then the loss of water was not, so they asked the Lord to provide water for them. They then began to praise him for doing so. Shortly, one of them turned on a faucet and water gushed from the well previously confirmed as dry.

Many students received the baptism in the Holy Spirit that weekend.

Notre Dame and Michigan State universities were also among the scenes of Holy Spirit experiences that winter and spring. The fire spread rapidly.

Bredesen, a leader in the worldwide charismatic renewal, planted the seed for the summertime community in Mount Vernon when he was invited to minister at Duquesne that winter. The excited young Christians were looking for an outlet for their enthusiasm, and such an ecumenical venture captured their imaginations.

Bredesen is a short, stocky, ebullient man with a shining face who almost literally bubbles over with wonder about following Christ. One of the first members of the established church to act and speak openly about the renewal, he has ministered around the world, from Japan to the Soviet Union, from Canada to Latin America, from Scandinavia to the Middle East, leading people literally by the thousands into a fuller life in Christ. In 1965 I became one of those thousands.

Most of the Catholic young people who joined the Mount Vernon community had a link to the Duquesne experience. The Protestants came from several sources. Some had been ministered to by Bredesen; some already worked for him in his rather freewheeling ministry based in that city; others had heard of the prospects for such a community by word of mouth.

So, together they came, to live in the Bredesen home as a Christian community—sleeping on the floor when necessary and eventually crowding Mrs. Bredesen and her children out and into the home of a friend for much of the time—and to spread the Gospel in that southernmost section of Westchester County.

It could have been any city anywhere. If Bredesen had been based in Chicago, and the Holy Spirit had moved in the same way, the community would have been in Chicago. But it was in Mount Vernon, New York, a city of more than 75,000, just over the line from the rapidly deteriorating borough of the Bronx. It had once been a wealthy and attractive suburban community in the famous and affluent county of Westchester, but with the spread of the metropolis it eventually fell to the blight and strife and suffering of most of America's cities. Much of the blame had fallen on the city's nonwhites, who made up a third of the population and were increasing in number as the wealthier whites moved farther into the country.

A day-by-day account of that summer in Mount Vernon would fill several volumes, each incident marvelous or horrible in its own way.

There was the beauty of the outreach of the young Christians into the parks and streets, the pizza parlors and bars, even the apartments and houses, of the unhappy city. The street people, mostly young, wandering and aimless, looking for anything they could grab hold of, whether good or bad, heard about Jesus Christ. It was relentless, but gentle. Older down-and-outers, drunkards, the lost, came face to face with someone who wasn't repulsed by them, someone who seemed to like them, someone who strangely asked them, "Do you know my Jesus?"

Bar owners ejected the young street witnesses, policemen became distressed over sidewalk gatherings (although they treated the Christian community with favor generally), and strongly denominational church people were upset by the indiscriminate mix of Christians from backgrounds that were traditionally considered incompatible. But day after day, night after night, the soft steps of these young followers of the Lord were heard covering the city.

There were no mass conversions, no big revival meetings, no headline-grabbing dramatics. It was sort of one on one, a gentle, personal witness, a patient expression of love.

The group learned quickly that the youth of that day wanted nothing to do with preaching in its conventional forms. They couldn't have cared less about traditional evangelism. But they did care about life, although many of them seemed to be selling it short. But if you had anything to say, they wanted it straight, direct. They wanted to *see* the truth. They didn't want clever dialogue, any fancy philosophy.

"You've got to come straight to the point," one of the girls in the group concluded after some time, "which is life with Jesus Christ. You've got to get them there quick. The best way is to get them to ask you something like, 'What are you so happy about?' And then you answer, 'Life.' They'll look at you for a second, and then you say, 'Life with the Lord.' Come right to the point. It's the only way."

I watched such directness work miraculously on two young men off the streets one night. They were good kids, but wild—scoffers, cynics. All that talk about God was a big joke. But the four young Christians stuck to the point—Christ crucified and resurrected, new life—and just when it seemed the situation was hopeless and even deteriorating, the two started to change. I couldn't believe my eyes.

The change began when the four witnesses realized deep down in their stomachs, rather than just in their minds, that they could do nothing. They literally, silently, turned the matter over to Christ. That silent prayer somehow generated power and in minutes those two not only were joining with the four in prayer, but also were laying hands on one another and praying for the Lord to come into their hearts "and don't come out."

I realized my head was wagging from side to side in wonder and I chuckled. It was then I noticed I'd been holding my breath. Such obvious intervention by the Holy Spirit was still a rarity for most of us.

A more bolt-like move by the Spirit came when a young lady of the world—a rather infamous woman virtually broken by a harsh, engulfing New York City society—arrived from Manhattan to encounter Jesus in the community's poor, simple prayer room without really intending to. As members of the group prayed in the Spirit—in ordinary language and in unknown tongues—she fell under painful conviction and ran from the room. She rambled almost incoherently that she had "never seen anything like that—they have something beautiful that I don't have—they have love all over their faces—"

That night she confessed her sins to Jesus Christ, embarking on the first wobbly steps of a new life.

Similarly, a student from a nearby Catholic seminary and several of his friends visited us one night. During prayer, one young Assembly of God fellow spoke rather loudly in tongues, and after twenty or thirty seconds the interpretation came through another person. Hardly three or four words had been spoken in the interpretation when the seminarian, who was kneeling, pitched forward on his face and began to sob deeply. He said later that, at that second, he had realized he really did not *know* the Lord—he had not fully given his life to Jesus Christ—a condition which he soon remedied. It was the presence of God, not merely what was being said in the tongues and interpretation, that had shown him his pitiable condition.

Yes, the personal outreach was remarkable. Few cities at that time had been privileged to see such love in action. But to me, really more of a counselor and observer than a participant, the Mount Vernon experience was two-edged, and I believe the most cutting edge, at least for that first summer, was the one within the group—the very existence of the community itself.

It was a witness to the world—although very small—that Protestants and Roman Catholics of all hues could come together under one roof, dedicated to one Lord, and overcome all obstacles of personality and background to reach out for Christ in a display of consuming love.

It was a love, an unjudging concern, that was unmistakable even to the most calloused.

"There is something there that you don't find any place else," an open-faced, good-looking young butcher asserted after encountering several of the people and attending one of their worship services. "You know it's from up there," he said, rolling his eyes toward the heavens. And this was a man who had at first been openly aggressive and almost hostile toward members of the community. He had even tried to entice one of the girl members to go with him to a motel. By midsummer, he was providing the community with its meat and other groceries, refusing to accept any payment.

And a priest from one of the local Catholic churches described the community as a place "where love is real." In fact, by the end of the summer he was spending several hours most days with the group, and sending to them a number of people needing help.

A real test of Christian love, quite expectedly, comes in maintaining order and propriety—in correcting a member of the body of Christ, for example. The natural man seems always either to use the bludgeon technique, destroying the offending individual, or to mimic the ostrich, hiding his head and ignoring flaws even though they might be ruining the individual's life and breaking down the community. The spiritual man, however, is supposed to love enough to run the risks of correction—but never with oppression—for the sake of the individual and the larger body.

There were several instances of such reproval. The sweetness of it was strange in the bitter world.

One case involved the hurt feelings of the youngest member, who was fourteen years old. Sullenness followed hurt feelings and active meanness followed sullenness. All of it grew out of youthful pride and a mistaken feeling of rejection that stemmed simply from the fact that he was younger than the others and didn't want to be. He wasn't as mature as the others but expected to speak with the voice of maturity. Quiet but firm counseling with two older members—and a lot of prayer together—soon restored the youngster to very significant usefulness within the body.

I was keenly aware during communal times of eating, praying, reading the Bible, or seeking God's will for the day or night, that we were not being counseled and comforted by mere human love—as real as that can be—but rather by a love outside the narrow limits of men. A poet might describe it as a warm, clean security that creeps over the senses like the fragrance of a red rose. Another might find in it the certainty of perfect existence that flows over a small, well-fed child as he is caressed by the warmth of his blankets on a cold winter's night.

I found in it specific evidence that God does in fact abide in men when they open their hearts—yield their minds and bodies—to him. My inner being hurt for the young people of those turbulent times who were forever staging "love-ins" or some other "happening" in the delusion that they were realizing love. They *did* long for love.

* * * *

Pulling all the threads together, summing up, was the most difficult part of the Mount Vernon experience. Even Bredesen, who had been involved with other followers of Jesus in wonder after wonder for a decade or more, found a summary elusive.

"It just seemed that miracle piled on top of miracle," he said, "and when you thought nothing could top the last one, then something else would happen. Look at the way the Lord led us together and then the way we overcame all kinds of personality differences to learn to live together, and how our food and everything we needed was provided by the Lord through the local businessmen and others.

"And then look at the way people have been drawn here through the community and the way the kids on the streets have responded to the street witnessing. No one would have thought it possible."

It was especially noteworthy that the compound of church, Sunday school building, and pastor's house, situated in the main area of racial unrest in the city, was not touched by the fighting and turmoil that swirled on every side. The only effect of the strife on the community's work was to inhibit its street witnessing for a few nights because of a police-imposed curfew.

Another noteworthy aspect of the experience was found in the stream of visitors that flowed through—clergymen and laymen of all denominations. Indeed, the group's most far-reaching testimony may have been presented through this stream. Consider this climactic event, which for me was perhaps the best example summarizing the community's work:

It was a clear, sunny Thursday. Arriving for the morning prayer were a mother superior and two other nuns who had traveled considerable distance by car. Following prayer and breakfast, Bredesen and I spent several hours with the three, sharing experiences and the Scriptures concerning the work of the Holy Spirit. We sat awhile in the church, then drove around the area on several errands, engrossed in fellowship. It was a time of extraordinary freedom of discussion and statement of opinion, of joyful excitement and confident expectancy. I had to admit, however, that I was a little uneasy inside. I had never had much to do with nuns.

Before the day was over, we were joined by three young people from the Duquesne group and we sort of slid into prayer as we sat in the old, stately church sanctuary. The church was the oldest in Mount Vernon.

After a few minutes, the three sisters asked the Lord to baptize them in the Holy Spirit. It was a strong, still moment—and a tense one for me. Five of us walked around to the pew behind the sisters and reached out to lay hands on them. "Is this okay to do?" I asked silently. I had never touched a nun before, and I was more than a little tentative.

I placed my hands on the head of the youngest of them and nearly fell over backwards when she immediately began to pray in tongues. The joyful language burst from her. I didn't know whether to shout hallelujah or to run. But it was magnificent. All three, by faith, were immersed in the Spirit of God by Jesus, filled with the Spirit, clothed with power from on high. They actually bubbled over with the Spirit.

It was a moment of glorious, golden unity as the two older Protestants—Harald and I—and the three young Roman Catholics laid hands on the three sisters, all knit together by the Holy Spirit.

As the young nun who had spoken in tongues so startlingly right in front of me left late that afternoon, she shook hands with Harald and then with me. Her eyes sparkled as she said, very modestly but very distinctly, "Praise the Lord!"

* * * *

Eleven years later, I leaned back in the chair in my study and thought about those 55,000 happy people at Giants Stadium. The Meadowlands had never known such a sweet presence.

What was this that God was doing? And how did it tie in with that little, unnoticed Mount Vernon experiment?

I picked up my Bible and thumbed toward the New Testament. St. John records for us the very touching plea of Jesus for his disciples, present and future, made to his Father as the hour of the cross approached:

"May they be brought to complete unity to let the world know that you sent me and have loved them even as you have loved me."[1]

Few verses have had more scrutiny in these days of great expectations. What time is being talked about? Has this occurred, and we failed to see it? No, that doesn't seem to stand up. The Lord said the world would be affected by it; it presumably would be visible. The world that he loved[2] would see that love.

Other Bible translations help to round out for us the very tantalizing words "complete unity." The King James Version says it beautifully: "perfect in one." And the Revised Standard Version is good: "perfectly one." The Living Bible says, "perfected into one," and finally the New American Standard Version lays it bare: *"perfected in unity."*

It would seem apparent then, as we look from this present moment back through church history, that we have not seen the fulfillment of the Lord's request. The church—and there is only one—has certainly not been brought to "complete unity." We certainly are not living the words of the great creeds handed down to us by the church fathers: "I believe one holy Catholic and Apostolic Church," "I believe . . . in the holy Catholic Church"[3]—although the statement of principle is true and worthy of our repetition.

But we, or our descendants, will see it come to pass one day if that Bible verse and the creeds are truly inspired, as most Christians believe. The Son will not be denied by the Father, for he did his work.

Even now, the wind is blowing. Let us see if we can trace its path.

CHAPTER TWO

In Back of the Wind

Nicodemus of the Bible,[1] although highly placed, was just an ordinary man who shows us much about ourselves as we look to see just who and what this wind of God is that we feel blowing in our midst. First, we easily identify with him. He came to Jesus at night, which we see as a reasonable move for a man in his position, and he came charitably, demonstrating a respect for this very unusual Man who was beginning to make extraordinary claims about himself and God. True, that respect may have been a bit patronizing, but on the other hand one has to be courteous.

Second, we smart under what looks like a rather rude rebuff to Nicodemus's opening remarks, which surely deserved some acknowledgment. Jesus ignored him, or so it seems, and set off on a new tack and utterly baffled Nicodemus. For a moment we thoroughly sympathize with him; he seems like a pretty nice guy. And he persevered; he didn't walk away mad.

What we don't see immediately is that the Lord felt there was no justification for Nicodemus's ignorance. After all, he was a leader of God's chosen people, a religious man. Didn't he understand that a person expecting to enter the kingdom of God had to be "born of the water and the Spirit"; that the experience was to be internal as well as external? Why didn't he know that? Why didn't he understand the Spirit better?

"You should not be surprised at my saying, 'You must be born again,' " Jesus said. "The wind blows wherever it pleases. You hear its sound, but you cannot tell where it comes from or where it is going. So it is with everyone born of the Spirit."[2]

"How can this be?" Nicodemus asked, and we fully identify with him in his ignorance.

"Can the Spirit really do what he wills?" we ask. "Is he really that free—like God?"

"Of course there's the doctrine of the Trinity," we say very naively, "but can this really be?"

And that was the way so many of us were in the early days of the marvelous renewal we are living through— just like Nicodemus—although we didn't all express it the same way obviously. The Scriptures, our heritage, even our experience in many cases, were so full of the truth of the Spirit, who blows like the wind, and yet we didn't see it.

* * * *

The first sentences of the Bible speak of this wind of God, the Holy Spirit:

In the beginning *God* created the heavens and the earth.[3]

The Hebrew for that first use of the name of God is *Elohim*, which is a plural word, suggesting that the writer understood the Creator as a God of multifaceted majesty and glory. But perhaps he understood him somehow as one God but consisting of more than one person. Knowledgeable .people disagree on which of these understandings the author of Genesis intended. But it seems logical that he was immediately pointing at that great mystery flowing through the whole Bible, right to the end, of God Almighty who is Three in One.

To me, the use of the plural, with the benefit of all the Scripture following, suggests a Godhead in which there is both unity and equality. At least there is a hint of this. And immediately out of the unity and equality comes a most mysterious, spine-tingling image of a member of that Godhead in action:

Now the earth was formless and empty, darkness was over the surface of the deep, and *the Spirit of God was hovering over the waters.*[4]

Having the magnificent gift of all the Scripture that follows, right through the Revelation, we tend to read much into that spellbinding passage that might not be there for one not having access to the remaining canon. But, benefiting from that gift, with all its unity and completeness, we have a glimpse of the enigmatic Godhead at work. Out of the unity and the equality flows the purpose of God—the creation.

We don't have to read far to find this suggested again. As God considers the creation of man—his finest work—we see the writer specifying plurality in the conversation within the Godhead:

Then God said, "Let *us* make man in *our* image, in *our* likeness."[5]

From the unity and agreement of the Godhead comes action.

Thus throughout the Old Testament we see the three persons of the Trinity, including the Spirit, working in unity but carrying out different functions—a fact that was to prove increasingly significant as the renewal progressed. For the accounts immediately remind one of St. Paul's words in his first letter to the Corinthians. Here he speaks of the diversity that often exists within unity:

> There are *different* kinds of gifts, but the same Spirit. There are *different* kinds of service, but the same Lord. There are *different* kinds of working, but the same God works all of them in all men.[6]

So it is apparently within the Godhead—equality and unity, yet diversity.

Passage after passage within the book of Isaiah speaks of the coming Messiah, the servant, the Root of Jesse, and it so often speaks of the simultaneous work of the Spirit in conjunction with the work of that Messiah, the Son.

Ezekiel in particular tells of the work of the Father, the Son, and the Spirit that Jesus felt Nicodemus should have understood better. He is speaking for God when he says:

> "For I will take you out of the nations; I will gather you from all the countries and bring you back into your own land. I will sprinkle clean water on you, and you will be clean; I will cleanse you from all your impurities and from all your idols. I will give you a new heart and put a new spirit in you; I will remove from you your heart of stone and give you a heart of flesh. And I will *put my Spirit in you and move you* to follow my decrees and be careful to keep my laws."[7]

Also, during Ezekiel's vision of the valley of dry bones—the bones being the people of God—the Lord

God says,

"I will *put my Spirit in you and you will live.*"[8]

It would seem clear, then, that Nicodemus—and indeed all of us—should have seen more readily that this internal work of the Spirit would be required for the new birth of God's people.

* * * *

Furthermore, we of the twentieth century have the many New Testament clarifications of just who this Holy Spirit is. For example, we see even more plainly near the close of Matthew's Gospel that the Scripture teaches the equality and unity of the Trinity:

Therefore go and make disciples of all nations, baptizing them in *the name* of the Father and of the Son and of the Holy Spirit.[9]

"The name" is singular. The Father, the Son, and the Holy Spirit have one name—God. They are a unity.

From there, we can quickly see in St. Paul's writings the thorough identification that the Lord Jesus Christ has with the Holy Spirit, who has a few verses earlier been described as the giver of life.[10]

But whenever anyone turns to the Lord, the veil is taken away. Now *the Lord is the Spirit*, and where the Spirit of the Lord is, there is freedom. And we, who with unveiled faces all reflect the Lord's glory, are being transformed into his likeness with ever-increasing glory, which comes from *the Lord, who is the Spirit.*[11]

While being separate personalities, they are so unified and of one essence as to both bear the name of Lord, which is translated from the Greek word *kurios,* meaning supreme in authority, Lord, master. But the two, Christ and the Spirit, have different functions in the overall purpose of the one God.

It is good to remember that the incarnate Lord said he could do nothing by himself, but only what he saw the Father doing,[12] and then later said that the Spirit, speaking nothing by himself, would reveal the things of Jesus.[13] But it was the Father who drew the people to Jesus in the first place.[14]

It is clear: The three yield to one another and serve one another for the glory they all share. And there is action in their unity.

That action is the specialty, so to speak, of the Holy Spirit. As we've seen, he might be described loosely as "the working arm of God on earth today"—remembering always that he is God. He is not merely a delegate.

In performing that work, which for the most part is done in and through people, he is quite rightly seen in terms of power—the power of God. He seems first to work in people and then to work through them. St. Paul himself put it in those terms of power:

> My message and my preaching were not with wise and persuasive words, but with a *demonstration of the Spirit's power*, so that your faith might not rest on men's wisdom, but on God's power.[15]

The Spirit, then, who has existed from the beginning, deals in power—power in and among people—and it was that with which the Christians of the charismatic renewal had to come to grips, as we shall see.

CHAPTER THREE

God's Heart Problem

Ever since he began to have anything to do with a people of his own, God has had something of a heart problem. It really isn't his problem; it's his people's. But he's made it his. And it's this problem, or traces of it, I am certain, that stands in the middle of the highway leading to the fulfillment of Christ's request for complete unity for his people. It is so basic that Christians in the charismatic renewal tend to forget it, but it undergirds everything.

The writer of the letter to the Hebrews gave a strong warning about the heart problem. He said this about God, quoting the Holy Spirit:

"Today, if you hear his voice, *do not harden your hearts* as you did in the rebellion."[1]

This was a warning issued three times in a chapter and a half.

It was the hard heart, according to the writer, that kept the people from entering into God's rest, into their inheritance. They would not cross the River Jordan because of their hardness.

In the cold, hard days of the late twentieth century,

the image of the hard heart is particularly appropriate. We in this time know first-hand the icy, steel hardness that can grip men. We understand hardheartedness, stiff-neckedness, brittleness, even in the church. Yes, we can feel the mean, unyielding hardness creeping into our own hearts as we do what we perceive to be the work of the Lord. I, as a writer, can faithfully pound out books and articles, can lecture informatively on the glory of the Lord, and can still know the deepening paralysis of hardness and coldness in my heart. First there comes aloofness from people and inevitably aloofness from God, even though we may deny this. There are many patterns.

Then, seeing our frozen condition, we read the words of St. Paul, and we weep:

> We have spoken freely to you, Corinthians, and opened wide our hearts to you. We are not withholding our affection from you, but you are withholding yours from us. As a fair exchange—I speak as to my children—*open wide your hearts also.*[2]

That great man had opened his mighty heart wide to God and to the people. It was open and pliable, receiving and giving. But the Christians, people like us, did not always reciprocate. Why?

It's good to go back to the beginning and take a fast, hopscotching journey through the history of God's dealings with his people to obtain a fuller understanding of the magnitude of that heart problem and the response to it. This has been a necessary exercise, in one form or another, for the people in the charismatic renewal, for the renewal hinges upon that response.

* * * *

God, according to the Bible, began his move upon a

people with his call to Abram, as recorded in Genesis. Essentially, it was an unconditional call, a unilateral move, wherein he set no *quid pro quo*, asked no one's permission, yet promised the richest blessing one could imagine. The only thing he seemed to require of Abram was to "go."

The Lord had said to Abram, "Leave your country, your people and your father's household and go to the land I will show you.

"I will make you into a great nation
  and I will bless you;
I will make your name great,
  and you will be a blessing.
I will bless those who bless you,
  and whoever curses you I will curse;
and all peoples on earth
  will be blessed through you."
So Abram left. . . .[3]

A land, a people, and a blessing were promised to him. He had an inheritance. God had simply moved upon him, externally, to begin calling out a people of his own—to begin remedying the effects of the Fall in the Garden of Eden.

Then, a bit later, the scriptural record shows a broadening of that first unconditional move upon our spiritual forefather. It remained external; God merely went ahead and moved upon a people. But conditions, the need for a response, began to appear.

When Abram was ninety-nine years old, the Lord appeared to him and said, "I am God Almighty; *walk before me and be blameless.* I will confirm my covenant between me and you and will greatly increase your numbers."[4]

The promise was still there, but Abram was not to live in just any old way; he was to walk with God, the only God. There was an obligation.

Abram fell facedown, and God said to him, "As for me, this is my covenant with you: You will be the father of many nations. No longer will you be called *Abram;* your name will be *Abraham,* for I have made you a father of *many* nations."[5]

Externals count for something with God—even a name. Throughout biblical history, names had a significance. The person *was* the name. Until God moved upon him, our forefather was Abram, "exalted father," but because of what God was making him, he became Abraham, "the father of many, a multitude." He *was* the name; the name *was* he.

I will make you very fruitful; I will make nations of you, and kings will come from you. I will establish my covenant as an everlasting covenant between me and you and your descendants after you for the generations to come, *to be your God and the God of your descendants after you.* The whole land of Canaan, where you are now an alien, I will give as an everlasting possession to you and your descendants after you; and *I will be their God.*[6]

God was making a covenant with Abraham and his descendants. It had one fundamental purpose: to make him their God and them his people. And it would be so down through the centuries, even to the present day, when, according to Scripture, the Christians would be reckoned among the children of promise, the "children of Abraham."[7] The Genesis account continues:

Then God said to Abraham, "As for you, you must

keep my covenant, you and your descendants after you for the generations to come. This is my covenant with you and your descendants after you, the covenant you are to keep: Every male among you shall be circumcised. You are to undergo circumcision, and it will be the *sign* of the covenant between me and you. For the generations to come every male among you who is eight days old must be circumcised, including those born in your household or bought with money from a foreigner—those who are not your offspring."[8]

God had moved upon his people and it had an external effect, an external response. There was to be a *sign* or seal of the relationship, something visible, something worked out physically. It was sort of a rite of admission to that group called God's people. Many Christians see it as a forerunner of baptism, with both rites representing the same promise, the only difference being purely external, thus justifying infant baptism.

Up to that point, except for some generalities that would take on more precise meaning as God's revelation progressed, the burden of this marvelous covenant seemed to fall pretty much on God. Abraham and his people just moved along faithfully—enjoying the ride, one might say.

But, as they moved along with their God, stumbling a lot, and grumbling even more, it became increasingly apparent that there was an internal side to this external work of God. A good summary of the unfolding complexities is found in the book of Deuteronomy, skipping over numerous significant stages in God's dealing with his people, including the giving of the Ten Commandments—the Law—that most crucial external expression of God's will. We pick up the account with Moses speaking:

> And now, O Israel, what does the Lord your God
> ask of you but to fear the Lord your God, to walk in
> all his ways, to love him, to serve the Lord your
> God with all your heart and with all your soul, and
> to observe the Lord's commands and decrees that I
> am giving you today for your own good?[9]

By then, it seems, with the giving of the Law, the
Lord was asking a great deal from his people, the
people of the covenant. It appears that he expected a
lot more than an external sign or seal.

As a child of Abraham through faith, I find myself
imagining my own reaction to those words, which
must have seemed so difficult. After all, they were just
ordinary people like us—grumblers, complainers. We
in this twentieth-century renewal often forget that.

"He wants me to fear him—to revere him?" I can
hear myself asking, my voice rising rather indignantly.
"He wants me to walk in *all* his ways? What in the
world does that mean? He wants me to *love* him? How
does anyone love God, someone you can't even see? How
do you serve him? Follow his commands? How?"

Being very fallible and very natural, I can see how
my first response to those two verses would be one of
dismay. "Ugh! It can't be done." Then, very quickly, I
would find anger seeping into the "woe-is-me" attitude.
And I hear myself saying rather rudely, "Just who
does God think he is to be asking such things of me?"

If I read on, I see very quickly just who he is and
what rights he has:

> To the Lord your God belong the heavens, even the
> highest heavens, the earth and everything in it.[10]

And again I mutter, "Ugh!" followed by a gulp. For the reply is strong. *"Everything* is mine," he is saying flatly, "including you. I can do anything I want."

Fortunately, as I read on, any harshness evaporates, taking my anger along with it.

> Yet the Lord set his affection on your forefathers and loved them, and he chose you, their descendants, above all the nations, as it is today.[11]

He is not saying it then because he has the right or because he is tough and harsh. He is saying it out of love. He is telling me to do those things because they're good for me, obviously. But still I ask in dismay, "How can I do those impossible things?"

And then comes the answer. It is as though he is saying, "If you want to do those first two verses, then do this verse."

> *Circumcise your hearts*, therefore, and do not be *stiff-necked* any longer.[13]

The word "stiff-necked" causes me to wince. Stiff-necked, stubborn—those are people words. They hit home. Then, for a second, I breathe easier as I get the point: It's a matter of the heart. It's internal, not just external.

But the relief lasts only a moment. "How in the world do you circumcise your heart?" My racing mind conjures up all kinds of ugly, gory images.

Fortunately, the revelation doesn't stop there, or the frustration would be overwhelming. There is hope further on in the same book as God increased the enlightenment of his people:

> *The Lord your God will circumcise your hearts*

and the hearts of your descendants, so that you may love him with all your heart and with all your soul, and live.[14]

I exhale loudly in my relief. "*He's* going to do it." He has demanded that I love him and now he's going to make that possible—all so I can *live.*

In that moment of tender fantasy as an Old Testament child of Israel, realizing finally that he wants me to live, I push aside a remaining tiny cloud of puzzlement to bask in God's concern for his people. As I peruse the following pages, I come to a passage that allows me to wallow in even more compassion. Moses is still speaking:

> This day I call heaven and earth as witnesses against you that I have set before you life and death, blessings and curses. Now *choose life,* so that you and your children may live and that you may love the Lord your God, listen to his voice and hold fast to him. *For the Lord is your life,* and he will give you many years in the land he swore to give to your fathers, Abraham, Isaac and Jacob.[12]

He is actually appealing to me in behalf of God to choose life. God is virtually pleading with me to choose him. "Come on, my children," he is saying, "don't be foolish; choose the blessing so that you can hold fast to me, so you can cleave to me, and be mine and I yours." It is very tender.

* * * *

But the tiny cloud is still there as my reverie shifts and moves on. "How is God going to circumcise my heart and soften up my stiff neck and stubborn will?"

With God there is no concern about time, a fact discerned in the whole flow of Scripture and history.

There is a fullness of time for everything, and the Lord is in no hurry. In this case, the time of the Law had its course to run; the pitiful condition of man as measured by that Law was to become painfully evident.

The Old Testament is laden with that evidence, as is secular history. Man's heart condition was worsening. And the people of God were not far behind, moving farther and farther from the will of their deliverer until the time when even they didn't truly comprehend what it meant to be the people of God.

It must be remembered that in the Old Testament the vast majority of God's people, the people of Israel, even though circumcised, were far from God. They bore the evidence of God's external move upon them, but nothing had occurred internally.

This is not alien to the Christian condition of the final years of the twentieth century, even in the midst of a remarkable renewal. If we are honest, we can see that, although our church rolls are fat and the pews are often filled, we as a people are truly far from God. We have received the rites of admission—even baptism—but in so many cases it has remained an external sign. The heart hardens, and the stiff-neckedness tightens.

In the case of the people of Israel, it finally reached the point described so painfully in the book of Jeremiah. One can almost hear the heart cry of God:

"The days are coming," declares the Lord, "when I will punish all who are circumcised only in the flesh—Egypt, *Judah*, Edom, Ammon, Moab and all who live in the desert in distant places. For all these nations are really uncircumcised, and even *the whole house of Israel is uncircumcised in heart.*"[15]

Things could not get much worse. It was the "whole house." After all that the Lord God, who chose them in love, had done for them—after all the deliverance, the provision, the direction—the people were inwardly cold toward him. They had the form of religion, but little else, and even that form was corrupted and perverted.

It's little wonder that people in the renewal, as they have discovered and rediscovered the Scripture, have seen tears on those pages. One of the tenderest cases of this in my experience involved Susan Atkins of the notorious Manson family. She was languishing in the Special Security Unit of the California Institution for Women, having virtually destroyed her life in the horror that filled and poured from the Manson gang. She had been convicted for a role in eight murders and had done just about everything else ugly and gross one could do. Her life seemed wiped out.

But in one of the age's most powerful acts of mercy, God determined otherwise. Through the written witness of a friend, Susan began to read the Bible. Since it was a book, she quite logically began at the beginning, not knowing that the traditional Christian approach is to concentrate at first on the New Testament.

It wasn't long before she found herself sitting on her bed in her cell one day, struggling with the unusual language of the King James Bible while tears rolled down her cheeks. "How could those people treat God like that?" she asked into the air.

While we worked together on a book about her life, *Child of Satan, Child of God,* she told me about those few moments.

"As I sat staring at the wall, I could feel the tears on

my face," she said. "I was weeping—weeping for God. 'Who am I to cry for God?' I thought. 'How presumptuous can you get?' I was suddenly confused. I was too small and inadequate for such emotions. I was furious at those people for turning their backs on this wonderful God and sinning right there in his presence."

She looked at me for a second and her soft brown eyes got very wide. Just a touch of a smile showed on her lips. "Suddenly the bomb fell. I saw something clearly for the first time. I was just like those children of Israel!"

Susan is one of the few people I know whose conversion to Jesus Christ grew out of the Old Testament. But she was granted the grace to see the hardness of heart, the cruel coldness that can come to people—even a people who have moved toward God outwardly. Her own hardness of heart was remedied shortly after this discovery.

* * * *

It is possible to trace God's heart problem with his people through all the pages of the Old Testament, but it seems that the point is established well enough by Jeremiah to permit moving into the New Testament. There we see it set forth again and even expanded, most clearly by young Stephen the martyr in the book of Acts. He was berating the leaders of the Jews for their blindness to what God was doing in the earth:

"You stiff-necked people, with uncircumcised hearts and ears! You are just like your fathers: You always *resist the Holy Spirit!*"[16]

It was a strong word, and it led to his death, but new light was cast on God's purpose. First, it is interesting to note the linking of the heart and ears. Apparently the heart gets hard, the neck gets stiff, and the hearing gets dull.

But most important is the adding of a wholly new factor—the Holy Spirit. Furthermore, he seems to be at the center of the issue; his role is not peripheral.

Fortunately, the unity of the Scripture, its wholeness—something many of us in the charismatic renewal have had to learn about—brings forth an elaboration and the mystery evaporates further. St. Paul contributed to this effectively in his letter to the Romans:

A man is not a Jew if he is only one *outwardly*, nor is circumcision merely outward and physical. No, a man is a Jew if he is one *inwardly;* and *circumcision is circumcision of the heart, by the Spirit,* not by the written code.[17]

The issue seems to come clear quickly. A relationship with God is not only external, but also internal. God seemingly moves upon people outwardly *and* inwardly. And the former is not effective without the latter.

The internal move is described as a "circumcision of the heart," and it is accomplished by the Spirit. Without it, the circumcision of the flesh is impotent; it is only a sign. It is God's will to provide the invisible work and for man to accompany that with the visible work. That is the perfect way.

If the view holds that baptism superseded circumcision after the coming of Christ and that they both signified the same thing—that is, regeneration—then it would seem permissible to take those two verses from Romans and substitute "Christian" for "Jew" and "baptism" for "circumcision" to arrive at a clearer picture of the people of God in the present age.

A man is not a *Christian* if he is only one outwardly, nor is *baptism* merely outward and physical. No, a man is a *Christian* if he is one inwardly; and *baptism* is *baptism* of the heart, by the Spirit, not by the written code.

If that is reasonable, and it seems so, would it not be clear that we Christians have a serious obligation to make sure that every step be taken to guarantee that an internal work on the heart accompanies the sacrament of water baptism? If we baptize infants, as the Israelites circumcised infants, mustn't we as the family of God do everything humanly possible to prepare the way for that child to receive the inner working of the Spirit? For, if these Scriptures mean what we believe they do, the outward sign, left by itself, will deteriorate into hardness of heart and a falling away from the purpose of God. It will do nothing for the saving of the soul.

However, the promises of Scripture taken together ring clear that if the community of God's people is faithful in its commitment to raising its children in the love and admonition of the Lord, among other things, then God will be faithful ultimately in his part, the inward work.

And how does he do it? How does he solve the problem posed by St. Paul's bold declaration?

The solution is found in the letter to the Galatians:

Because you are sons, God *sent* the Spirit of his Son *into* our hearts, the Spirit who calls out, *"Abba,* Father."[18]

God himself, who said after he had called us out as his people, his children, that he would circumcise our hearts so we could truly be his people, accomplishes it with the Holy Spirit, the Spirit of Christ. In the renewal we found it was as though the Father sees us flopping about helplessly in our impotence and shoots the arrow of the Spirit right into our hearts, opening them wide, circumcising them. Zap! We are his and we know it, and we know all through our being that he is our Father. Before, we knew it outwardly, but now we know it through and through. We have been born again.

St. Paul expanded on this wonderful phenomenon at another point in his wide-ranging letter to the Romans:

. . . those who are led by the Spirit of God are sons of God. For you did not receive a spirit that makes you a slave again to fear, but you received the Spirit of sonship. And by him we cry, "*Abba*, Father." The Spirit himself testifies with our spirit that we are God's children. Now if we are children, then we are heirs—heirs of God and co-heirs with Christ, if indeed we share in his sufferings in order that we may also share in his glory.[19]

People in the renewal, indeed people for centuries, have found this to be one of the most beautiful revelations in Scripture. God himself penetrates the very essence of his people and testifies to them, again and again, that they *are* his people. He convinces them that they should call him Father, just as his only begotten Son did. In fact, it is the very same Spirit that dwelt in Jesus that resides in God's people and persuades them that they too, through adoption, might call him Father, even Daddy. Because it is the same

Spirit, they know that the Father hears his adopted children with the same sensitivity, the same willingness, with which he heard his beloved Son.

With that, cold, hard hearts melt, stiff, willful necks become pliable, and stubbornness gives way to yieldedness. Once-dull ears hear the words of their Lord:

. . . my yoke is easy and my burden is light.[20]

But experience showed us a pitfall. The heart must be attended to consistently; it must be kept open. Inattention can allow the soft, moist condition to become hard and dry. And dryness stiffens into brittleness. Even the most devoted and practiced child of God can, through carelessness, idleness, or misuse, allow his once-circumcised heart to harden into ineffectiveness. And it will bring tears to his eyes when he detects it. He does not intend for it to happen; indeed, it often happens when one seemingly is caught up in good works for the Lord, so caught up going one way that his neck becomes stiff, so committed to a position that he becomes stubborn. The Lord might make a turn and he will miss it altogether.

But, fortunately, there is a remedy for that, too, the same remedy provided for those coming to the Lord for circumcision of the heart for the first time. It is found in the words of Jesus:

"Which of you fathers, if your son asks for a fish, will give him a snake instead? Or if he asks for an egg, will give him a scorpion? If you then, though you are evil, know how to give good gifts to your children, how much more will your Father in heaven give the Holy Spirit *to those who ask him!*"[21]

If the Holy Spirit is the solution—and he certainly seems to be—he is available to do his work for the asking. And that was a central principle for the renewal. The relationship of God's people to their God is to be an "asking" one. God, who made and sustains everything, who is forever giving, desires that his people be forever asking, forever receiving. "I will be their God," he said, "and they will be my people."

A little game of acronyms—unfair but fun—makes the point of the "asking" relationship quite effectively. It, too, utilizes a well-known verse from Luke:

> "So I say to you: Ask and it will be given to you; Seek and you will find; Knock and the door will be opened to you."[22]

The acronym is A.S.K. Unhappily, the sentence was not spoken, nor recorded, in English.

Finally, we are given more detail on how that "asking" works out in opening the heart, both of the first-timer and the veteran believer. It comes in an old chestnut of a verse, used effectively for years in evangelism, even though the words were addressed to believers, presumably Spirit-filled believers:

> Here I am! I stand at the door and knock. If anyone hears my voice and opens the door, I will go in and eat with him, and he with me.[23]

They were words directed at God's people who had grown stale, lukewarm, neither hot nor cold. And they provide hope for those of us in the twentieth century who often find our hearts hard. True, the Lord by his Spirit comes into our hearts when we at last receive him at the time of our conversion. St. John, in his Gospel, described this as being "born again" or "born from above"—born of the Spirit. Jesus, as he does with all people, knocks and is ready to come into every life. But the verse means more than that. He will keep coming in, afresh as it were, day in and day out revealing more of himself, more of God's will, as we open the doors of our hearts. Reminding his people of the special times he revealed himself during the breaking of bread, during the sharing of a meal, during the Lord's Supper, he says he will come in by the Spirit time after time to sit down and eat with us.

And that is how the "asking" relationship works out, as so many in the renewal have been learning. That is how the hard heart is first circumcised. That is how the circumcised, but brittle, crusty heart is made pliable and responsive to God's will. That is how the wind blows.

But there are other breezes in that great wind, and people all over the land have been setting their sails for them in an unprecedented manner.

CHAPTER FOUR

Normality

I don't remember the exact date—it must have been in the mid-sixties—but I remember the impact when my eyes landed with a modicum of comprehension on a coldly sobering verse in St. John's Gospel. First there was disbelief. "You've got to be kidding!" I'm not sure I said the words aloud, but I might as well have. They were there.

I was reading the Revised Standard Version of the Bible; it was quoting Jesus:

"Truly, truly, I say to you, he who believes in me will also do the works that I do; and greater works than these will he do, because I go to the Father."[1]

I quickly whipped through the King James Version I kept on the bookshelf. It said the same thing, only in older language.

Today's modern translations say it even more starkly and can set one to trembling even more quickly:

"I tell you the truth, *anyone* who has faith in me will do what I have been doing."[2]

A couple of my favorite exclamations during those

early days of discovery were "ugh" and "ouch." And I still find myself using them as I read through the Scriptures.

If Jesus really said that and really meant it—and by that time I had no reason to think otherwise—then it was necessary to face it. Thousands like me were being forced to do the same thing, perhaps in different ways. It was obviously too important to ignore.

The statement is almost brutal in its force. For there's no way, it seems to me, that we can avoid looking at ourselves after reading it and asking, "Am I doing the works Jesus did, let alone greater works?"

The first thing we have to do, logic would dictate, is to dig into what Jesus was talking about. What did he mean when he spoke of his "works" or "what I have been doing"?

The best course would seem to be a check into what he said about himself. What did *he* think he came to do? And, right away, we find the perfect description in the Gospel according to Luke, once again experiencing the wholeness of the Scripture, the explanation that it gives of itself.

This time, clarification comes in a tender, moving passage that raises great images and visions as we look with the mind's eye. It follows right after the account of the Lord's temptation by the devil in the wilderness that came after his baptism by John and the descent of the Holy Spirit upon him:

> Jesus returned to Galilee *in the power of the Spirit*, and news about him spread through the whole countryside. He taught in their synagogues, and everyone praised him.[3]

Immediately we're struck with the recollection that

even Jesus, the Son of God, who was very much a man while being very much God, required the presence of the Spirit, apparently because of his manhood. And we're also struck by the realization that he went first to the synagogues, the churches of the day, God's people.

> He went to Nazareth, where he had been brought up, and on the Sabbath day he went into the synagogue, as was his custom.[4]

It's hard for us to envision the scene. We actually know so little. The synagogue was undoubtedly the finest place in town, but compared with more urban standards then and with the affluence of today it was probably small and poor, perhaps even crude. It was most likely dimly lighted, maybe even dark and gloomy. Most of the people—with women and men seated apart—were probably poor and their manner of dress reflected this status. The portable ark containing the scrolls of the Law and the prophets stood at one end, facing the entrance. In front of the ark and facing the worshipers, occupying the "chief seats," were the synagogue leaders. And in the center of the room stood the reading desk and platform.

Everything became very quiet.

> And he stood up to read. The scroll of the prophet Isaiah was handed to him. Unrolling it, he found the place where it is written:
> *"The Spirit of the Lord is on me,*
>   because he has anointed me
>   to preach good news to the poor.
> He has sent me to proclaim freedom for the prisoners
>   and recovery of sight for the blind,
> to release the oppressed,

to proclaim the year of the Lord's favor."[5]

We can almost feel the silence, the mystery of that moment—the held breaths, the fixed stares.

Then he rolled up the scroll, gave it back to the attendant and sat down. The eyes of everyone in the synagogue were fastened on him, and he said to them, "Today this scripture is fulfilled in your hearing."[6]

The pivotal statement in the passage right up to the end is "the Spirit of the Lord is on me." We can almost see him sweeping his hands from above his head down over his shoulders and upper body, acting out the invisible fact of the covering of the Spirit. He had been anointed with the Spirit, covered with the Spirit, which for a flashing moment by the River Jordan had earlier been seen as a descending dove accompanied by a voice that said:

"You are my Son, whom I love; with you I am well pleased."[7]

Flowing out of that covering declaration—"the Spirit of the Lord is on me"—is a poetic summation of the works of Jesus. Those are the things he came to do. But for those of us who might be lulled into a beautiful dullness by the tenderness of the passage, there are words to jolt us awake. We need only to turn a page or two and we find Jesus again summarizing his works. John the Baptist, in prison, has sent two of his followers to Jesus to ask if he really is the One.

So he replied to the messengers, "Go back and report to John what you have seen and heard: The blind receive sight, the lame walk, those who have leprosy are cured, the deaf hear, the dead are raised, and the good news is preached to the poor.

Blessed is the man who does not fall away on account of me."[8]

Once again, I find the word "ugh" escaping from my mouth. The works of Jesus are declared plainly, and the words of St. John haunt me—"greater works than these shall you do." How can that be?

Were it not for the careful explanations of Scripture I would certainly find myself slipping into despair. Armed with that key verse spoken by Jesus—"the Spirit of the Lord is on me"—I can find the way.

* * * *

Continuing in Luke's Gospel, we find over at the end a most critical piece of instruction. Jesus had been crucified and resurrected, and had appeared to his disciples. He presumably had already breathed on them, saying, "Receive the Holy Spirit."[9] Then St. Luke tells us this:

Then he opened their minds so they could understand the Scriptures. He told them, "This is what is written: The Christ will suffer and rise from the dead on the third day, and repentance and forgiveness of sins will be preached in his name to all nations, beginning at Jerusalem. You are witnesses of these things."[10]

The resurrected Christ gave them a capsule of the events of the Gospel (although we can be quite sure he spoke in greater detail than what St. Luke was inspired to write at this point), and then told them they were to bear witness to those events. But he also stopped them in their tracks with an unexpected command:

"I am going to send you *what my Father has promised*; but stay in the city until you have been *clothed with power from on high."*[11]

Phrases such as "the promise of the Father" occur several times in the New Testament, and they take on particular significance in light of these words of Jesus. Furthermore, they are here linked to another suddenly significant phrase, "clothed with power from on high," which immediately brings to mind the image of Jesus reading in the synagogue, "The Spirit of the Lord is on me." It would seem that "what my Father has promised" is related to, indeed is the same thing as, being "clothed with power from on high."

If one is a person of gestures, he is likely to find himself making the same motions when he says, "I am clothed with power from on high" that he makes when he says, "The Spirit of the Lord is upon me." The words seem to portray the same thing.

Keeping this Gospel passage in mind, we can follow through on the theme in another piece of writing by St. Luke—the book of Acts. He opened the latter work right where he closed the Gospel and in fact repeated several key elements:

> After his suffering, he showed himself to these men and gave many convincing proofs that he was alive. He appeared to them over a period of forty days and spoke about the kingdom of God. On one occasion, while he was eating with them, he gave them this command: "Do not leave Jerusalem, but wait for *the gift my Father promised,* which you have heard me speak about. For John baptized with water, but in a few days you will be *baptized with the Holy Spirit."*[12]

Once again Luke refers to the "promise of the

Father," and then adds the declaration that they will be "baptized with the Holy Spirit." The construction of the passage makes it plain that the "gift my Father promised" is equivalent to being "baptized with the Holy Spirit."

The injunction was perfectly clear: They—and we generally consider this to include all Christians—were to go into the world, preaching the Gospel. We all acknowledge this as the Great Commission, spoken so unequivocally at the end of three of the four Gospels and reinforced throughout the New Testament. But they were not to go until they had been clothed with power from on high, an act that Christ's words indicated was the normal expectation for his people. For if the Great Commission was for all Christians, then so was the power from on high. The fulfillment of the "promise of the Father" was part of the normal Christian life. Without the promise of the Father, they would be *subnormal* and had better not venture out lest they be devoured by the wolves. They would be impotent.

But with this promise of the Father, this clothing with power from on high, this baptism with the Holy Spirit, they would be like their Lord, who had said, "The Spirit of the Lord is on me, because he has anointed me. . . ." Jesus was the Christ, the anointed one. They would be little Christs, little anointed ones, which is a good definition for the term Christian.

Furthermore, the words of the Lord just before he ascended into heaven would certainly be real:

". . . you will receive power when the Holy Spirit comes on you; and you will be my witnesses in Jerusalem, and in all Judea and Samaria, and to the ends of the earth."[13]

When Jesus said to his disciples that before long they would be baptized with the Holy Spirit, he took them back to a statement of John the Baptist that is found in all four Gospels. For John had spoken plainly that the one who was coming after him—the Christ—would baptize with the Holy Spirit. John could only baptize with water. Man would not be able to do this mighty thing that he foresaw; only God could do it. And that's still the way it is. It's important for Christians to understand that this baptism with the Spirit is one of the ministries that Jesus did *not* pass along to his followers. He kept it for himself.

So when he said, "You will be baptized with the Holy Spirit," he was saying, "*I* will baptize you with the Holy Spirit." This follows God's pattern completely. Only he can bring people into the church—"we were all baptized *by one Spirit* into one body"[14]—and only God can empower us to serve him by baptizing us with or in his Spirit.

It's helpful to see how this baptism with the Spirit works, although in the renewal such understanding rarely preceded the experience. First, the Greek word here rendered "baptized" is *baptizo*, which means to immerse, to saturate, to make fully wet.

I remember talking to David du Plessis about the word once. "Well," he said, with that famous twinkle in his eye, "when you're talking about water and you use the word *bapto* you mean wet or covered with water, but when you say *baptizo*, you mean sunk—permanently."

So Jesus takes his follower in his hands like a little child and dips him, immerses him, in the Holy Spirit,

fully covering him, saturating him with the Spirit—
with power from on high. And at that point the follower has the Spirit within him—which is true of all believers—and he has the Spirit all over him. He is, in a
manner of speaking, bubbling over with the Spirit.
That explains why, in so many cases, the result is an immediately visible one, as it apparently was in the cases
of the people ministered to by St. Peter in Samaria[15]
and in Cornelius's household.[16]

* * * *

Susan Atkins once again provided a good illustration
of this marvelous transaction. Having been converted
to Christ while alone in her prison cell, just at the point
when it seemed her life was destroyed, she some weeks
later was praying, again alone in her cell. She had had
precious little instruction except for a few books, but
she had her Bible. And she was thoroughly convinced
of the reality of Jesus Christ because of what he had
already done to her. However, she was skittish—understandably hesitant in her aloneness—about this matter
of being "baptized with the Holy Ghost," as her King
James Bible said it.

But she opened her heart to her Savior and whis-
pered, "Dear Jesus, if you want to baptize me with the
Holy Ghost, here I am. Have your way. Make me willing
to take what you want to give to me."

As she lay in her bed in the nine-by-eleven cell, she
began to sense something washing over her, and she
felt as though she were floating. She opened her eyes,
but she was still in her bed. Yet she knew something
was happening. "I tingled all over," she said later, "and
I knew what it was. It was the love and the peace of
Jesus. It was washing over me, more intensely than on
the night of my conversion. . . . I began to feel a rising
sensation, as though I were rising in an elevator. . . .

"I held my breath for a moment. The wonderful rising sensation continued. I was being lifted up in huge, soft hands, higher, and higher. I was like a little baby in its father's hands. This time I kept my eyes closed—tight. I was rising. . . .

"Once again, I heard the voice of Jesus. It was unmistakable. But he wasn't talking to me this time. I knew he was talking to the Father. I couldn't understand the words, but I didn't care. . . ."

At that moment, she sensed somehow that Jesus, holding her in his "huge, soft hands" dipped her into the Holy Spirit like a little baby.

"I was immersed in love," she said.

Most of us don't have experiences quite that vivid, for a variety of reasons, but that is the sort of thing that happens to us when we are baptized with the Holy Spirit, even when we don't have such lively perceptions. We come up ready—and able—to be Christ's witnesses.

* * * *

The first chapter of Acts [17] offered some between-the-lines help for those people in the renewal who at first feared that this extraordinary empowerment by God's Spirit was only for those first disciples, a thought lacking in convincing scriptural support.

So when they [the disciples] met together, they asked him [Jesus], "Lord, are you at this time going to restore the kingdom to Israel?"[18]

Jesus had been telling of such marvelous things that they couldn't imagine the end time wasn't upon them. Surely, if Christ was going to do something as marvelous as this, the time for his visible reign must have been near. But the following sentences clear it up:

He said to them: "It is not for you to know the times

or dates the Father has set by his own authority. But you will receive power when the Holy Spirit comes on you. . . ."[19]

No, the end was not upon them. This marvelous gift of power—the gift of the Holy Spirit—was being made so they could be his witnesses until the end came. He was sending them into the age of the Spirit, the age of the church, and they were to have his power to carry on until his reign would become visible. We are still in that age today.

* * * *

I can remember lying in bed night after night shortly after my conversion in 1965 and wrestling with thoughts of the baptism in the Holy Spirit. What did one have to do to get ready? Was I ready? Was I worthy? All the trite thoughts were mine.

But fortunately in the Scriptures there are simple answers for those and other questions. One section that I found most helpful was the account of the first Christians' experiencing this baptism on the day of Pentecost.[20]

The setting was simple. The group of believers numbered about a hundred twenty, and they were all together on the day of Pentecost. The Spirit came upon them, sounding like a violent wind, and they were baptized in the Spirit—filled and covered with the Spirit— and they saw little flames of fire resting upon one another. They began to praise and worship God in a most unusual and powerful way. They even praised him in other tongues as the Spirit enabled them.

Apparently, in their great excitement and enthusiasm, they filed out of the upper room where they so often had gathered and wandered down into the streets, maybe to a square, where there were many people from many places. Amazingly, those people could hear the Christians praising God in foreign tongues, and they could understand them. It was quite a mob scene, with hundreds, even thousands, gathering around those remarkable Christians.

Then, at last, the apostle Peter—the one who had been so confused and fearful when Jesus was taken captive, the one who had lied and run, the one so human that most of us easily identify with him—stood forth with the eleven other apostles and delivered a discourse to the astonished bystanders. Christians refer to it as the first sermon. And in his words, we find the most thorough, the most solid teaching possible, on preparation for the baptism in the Holy Spirit.

For example, we read this:

"Men of Israel, listen to this: Jesus of Nazareth was a man accredited by God to you by miracles, wonders and signs, which God did among you through him, as you yourselves know. This man was handed over to you *by God's set purpose and foreknowledge*."[21]

Everything that happened to Jesus was done according to God's purpose and plan. It didn't happen willy-nilly. God sent Jesus to do what he did and to receive what he received. He was *sent*, being divine. Point number one.

". . . You, with the help of wicked men, *put him to death* by nailing him to the cross."[22]

Point number two: He was killed, *crucified*.

"But *God raised him from the dead*, freeing him from the agony of death, because it was impossible for death to keep its hold on him."[23]

Jesus, having been crucified, was raised from the dead, *resurrected*—point number three. Peter then talked at length about the resurrection and how it had been foreseen by King David, as reflected in the Psalms. Perhaps because the resurrection is so central to the Christian faith, he dwelt at length on it and then repeated his point:

"God has raised this Jesus to life, and we are all witnesses of the fact."[24]

Then he moved quickly to his fourth point:

"Exalted to the right hand of God, he has received from the Father *the promised Holy Spirit* and has poured out what you now see and hear."[25]

Having returned to his exalted place with the Father, Jesus had sent the promise of the Father to his people in a new and special way. *He had sent the Holy Spirit.*

And then, in one of the most resounding declarations ever made, the one to and from which all history flows, St. Peter drove home his fifth and final point:

"Therefore let all Israel be assured of this: God has made this Jesus, whom you crucified, both *Lord* and *Christ.*"[26]

Jesus, the anointed one, was *the Lord*! That was the clincher.

Thus big, burly Peter—the fisherman, the impetuous one—with marvelous articulation and courage in the face of a mob, laid down for all time the understanding required of any who would follow Jesus in the power of the Holy Spirit. They must know that Jesus was sent— he was divine; he was crucified for their sins; he was resurrected; he went to the Father and sent the Holy

Spirit as promised; and, most crucially, he was the Lord.

Anyone understanding and believing those truths is a candidate for the baptism with the Holy Spirit by Jesus Christ.

For me, the last point was a killer. To really know deep inside myself, and to be willing to live in that knowledge, that Jesus is absolute Lord was extremely difficult for me. Oh, I had been truly converted. I had assented—certainly intellectually—to the fact of his Lordship. But it seems that it was not a deep-rooted part of reality for me. It was inside me but not all over me, perhaps.

* * * *

I remember the day vividly—in the spring of 1965. I had been a professing Christian for one month to the day, and I yearned to experience the fullness of Christ in the way of other people I had been seeing. So I drove to Mount Vernon, New York, from my home in Ridgewood, New Jersey, and met with Harald Bredesen, the man who had led me to Christ in the first place.

"Harald," I said a bit too forcefully, "I know there's more, and I want it."

He smiled and put his arm around me and we went into the church. He knew me well enough to be convinced of my sincerity and understanding. So we began to pray and walk, walk and pray, up and down the center aisle of the old, dark church. We'd sit in one of the pews and talk about the Lord, then we'd get up and walk some more. We'd laugh. And we'd pray and walk.

But nothing seemed to be happening. I was becoming frustrated. Perhaps I really wasn't good enough! Perhaps the Lord didn't want me to be his witness!

I knew the Scripture well enough by then to understand that those were lies. I knew that none of us was really good enough, but that only by grace through faith were we saved, and I also knew that Jesus called all of his people to serve him. None was excluded.

At last, Harald and I sat down in the third pew from the front on the right, and I felt very low. "Just think about the Lord," Harald said. "Just think about what he's done for you."

In a few moments, an unusual thing happened. I felt as though I were crumbling into little pieces, thousands of them. My brittle, hard exterior was crumbling and falling onto the floor. At that moment, I knew and really believed that Jesus was the Lord. He was absolutely *the* Lord; there was no one up there on the throne but him—not me, not my wife, not my children, not my job. That last one—my job—was, oh, so hard to let go of. But I actually, sincerely wanted Jesus to be the Lord, which he already was of course.

As the crumbling continued, I began to cry, and then to sob. The sobs were deep, and they hurt. But I let the crumbling go on, mumbling, "Yes, Lord." I finally yielded.

In just a matter of moments, I began to pray more and more audibly, and the sobbing subsided. I was praying in an unknown language. It poured out. And I laughed. I'm afraid I shouted too. I prayed on and on. It was beautiful.

Harald prayed right along with me, and he laughed and shouted too.

I had a sense—it might even be properly called a vision—as this was occurring that I was at the bottom of a quite long shaft, probably a well shaft. It all happened very quickly, but I later remembered it clearly in all its parts, in a sort of slow motion, and I've never forgotten it. I was looking up the shaft, and the mouth of it was probably twelve or fifteen feet away. There, just above the mouth, was a small cage. It held a bird. I was unusually inexperienced in Christian figures in those days and thought of the bird as a pigeon. When I got the hang of things a little better later on, I could see that it obviously was a dove. But, at any rate, this bird was being squeezed unmercifully by the cage. The bars were pressing in on its wings and it couldn't move.

As this process of crumbling and sobbing and unknown tongues reached its climax, I "saw" the walls of the cage pull back, and back, and back, right out of sight, and the bird was able to move its wings, to fly, to soar—just as it was intended to do.

That, I knew, was what had happened to me. I was free, and able to soar.

It helped me to appreciate this vision sometime later when I read the powerful words of Psalm 124. They affirmed my experience:

Praise be to the Lord,
  who has not let us be torn by their teeth.
We have escaped like a bird
  out of the fowler's snare;
the snare has been broken,
  and we have escaped.
Our help is in the name of the Lord,
  the Maker of heaven and earth.[27]

With the freedom came the power to be what God had intended when he first made me a follower of his Son—a witness. And what is a witness? He is evidence—evidence of the love and life of Christ manifested in a variety of ways, in a variety of styles. Sometimes he is dynamic; sometimes he is not. Sometimes he is vocal; sometimes he is not. But he is always evidence, because the power of God dwells within him and rests upon him.

But how does it work out? What happens next? I and millions like me were to find out.

CHAPTER FIVE

Power to Do Something

I was sitting in the second row on the left of the First Reformed Church in Mount Vernon that early-summer day in 1965. Thirty or more of us had gathered for the regular vesper service and we began with a half-hour of free prayer. Some sat in brightly colored, canvas-backed chairs near the pulpit, facing the pews; others sat in the pews, some singly, some in irregular clusters. My wife was on my right; others were on each side of us.

Harald Bredesen's words, spoken quietly just before the service began, seemed stuck in my mind. "I believe the Lord wants to speak through you today, brother." His bright smile failed to stop the tremor of fear that rippled through me.

I had been a Christian only a couple of months. I was wholly inexperienced and unschooled in such matters, and my knowledge of the Bible was very meager. How could I have anything to say?

Still, I wanted so much to be like the Christians I was encountering. They spoke so eloquently, it seemed to me, and they were so free and loving. Bible verses and words of wisdom fairly dripped from their lips.

I was extremely nervous as I listened to others pray and occasionally chimed in with a "thank you, Lord," or a "praise you, Jesus." I admired those who could sustain a lengthy, meaningful prayer. I could manage only a few sentences at a time. I was actually beginning to tremble in my nervousness, starting inside with a jelly-like feeling and moving outside to downright shaking. Harald's words became louder inside my head. I wanted him to be right, but I was terrified.

My eyes were closed, and things became quiet. Suddenly, I bolted to my feet, eyes still closed and hands clenched tightly. I don't know why I stood; it just seemed like the right thing to do. I had nothing on my mind except for one word—"you." I had been told to blurt out what was on my mind, and that's what I did.

"You—you've—got to come out of the cracks!"

That's all there was. "There must be more," I thought in panic. I strained, and my scalp tightened. My face muscles were like rocks. What was I going to do?

I repeated the sentence. "You've got to come out of the cracks."

I sat down heavily, embarrassed, humiliated. I put my face in my hands on my knees, and I wept. I had failed. I had wanted to participate in the ministry, and I had tried to show off. I had failed.

The prayers continued as though nothing had happened, and there was great joy in the singing and the handclapping. But I was miserable. I didn't look at anyone for a long time, and no one said anything about my "prophecy."

* * * *

It was nearly six months later. I had continued to

attend the Sunday evening vesper services off and on, but was sidetracked by other activities many times. After one fairly prolonged absence, Gloria and I returned that day and rejoiced at the remarkable spontaneity of the group, which was considerably enlarged by new people. That meeting was a watering place for many thirsty Christians in those early, fragile times.

The meeting proceeded pretty much as usual—good singing, good prayers, prophecy from several men and women. And then there were testimonies. One woman a few seats back, toward the middle of the sanctuary, got to her feet and said, rather softly and timidly at first, "I'd like to speak a word about how mysteriously the Lord works. Most of you don't know me, but I'm from Hartford, and I've only been here once before— several months ago. Well, that day that blond-haired man over there"—I looked up and she was pointing at me—"got up and said just a few very unusual words."

She smiled, but there were tears in her eyes. "He said, 'You've got to come out of the cracks.' He probably had no idea what that meant, or how important it was, but those words went into my heart like a knife."

She paused and looked straight at me. "I had been living in the cracks—in my own church. I had been hiding in the cracks—like a mouse—like someone afraid."

Again she stopped, then pressed on. "I had been touched by the Lord before. I had had a very special encounter with him, and he had filled me with his Spirit, but still I was hiding. I didn't tell anyone, I didn't share with anyone—I just kept it to myself—and meanwhile my church was dying. It was just drying up. The people—my friends—were losing their faith, and there was no life there. But I hid in the cracks. I didn't try to do anything to help. I was too shy."

She looked down for a second and then back up. A smile covered her face. "But those strange-sounding words—'You've got to come out of the cracks'— revolutionized my life. I've come out of the cracks, out of my complacency, and I've started to tell people about Jesus. And things are a lot better."

She smiled again, and sat down.

I was struck dumb, but I know my face shone like a bare light bulb. I couldn't stop my mouth from turning up at the corners, but neither could I stop the tears in my eyes. Harald was looking at me; so was Gloria. They looked like light bulbs too. They knew what I had felt six months earlier.

God had actually spoken out of the mouth of a babe. It wasn't the perfect way for a prophet, as later experience was to show, but it had been a beginning. It had gotten the job done.

* * * *

That's the way it has been in the charismatic renewal. People have come to the Lord, been baptized in the Spirit, and gone on to serve him and his people in one way or another. They have been born from above, been clothed with power from on high, and experienced manifestations of the Spirit to help meet the needs of others.

Some have not learned the lesson easily. It has been difficult for them to see that all Christians are called to serve the Lord, to minister. Jesus first says, "Come," and then he says, "Go." His people are first "called out" and into his church—the "called-out ones"—and they are "set apart" or consecrated; they are holy. Then they are "sent out" to be witnesses, some close by, some far away.

The thing most of us have had trouble with is understanding that God never sends anyone out without empowering him. Oh, many go out without being empowered, but God never *sends* them that way. God *never* commissions without equipping. If we believe we have a mission—and all Christians have one—then we can be sure we will be given the ability to accomplish that mission.

The problem in the renewal was that many of us heard the call and commission but then lost the assurance that God would do his part if we went. We became afraid, even panicky. We often balked, and asked God to send someone else.

There's a lot of background for that reaction. We have only to look at some of the stalwarts in the Bible.

Moses is a good example. Early in the book of Exodus we find God saying,

> "So now, go. I am sending you to Pharaoh to bring my people the Israelites out of Egypt."[1]

Moses immediately misses the point, looks at himself, and tries to back out:

> "Who am I, that I should go to Pharaoh and bring the Israelites out of Egypt?"[2]

And so it goes, verse after verse. Moses continually fails to hear God saying, "I will be with you," and he makes excuse after excuse until finally he blurts out:

> "O Lord, I have never been eloquent, neither in the past nor since you have spoken to your servant. I am slow of speech and tongue."[3]

Seemingly exasperated, God fires back,

"Who gave man his mouth? Who makes him deaf or dumb? Who gives him sight or makes him blind? Is it not I, the Lord? Now go; I will help you speak and will teach you what to say."[4]

And finally, Moses, who we must remember was merely a man like us, falls completely apart in his doubt and sobs,

"O Lord, please send someone else to do it."[5]

We read that the Lord's anger burns against Moses and he turns to Aaron, Moses' brother.[6]

Moses, the great man of God, was unable to believe that, no matter how great the obstacle, *with the call comes the power.* But he wasn't the only one. There was Jeremiah.

In the first chapter of his great prophecy, we see God calling him to be his prophet, his mouthpiece, having set him apart before he was born. But immediately Jeremiah looks at his frailty and tries to beg off:

"Ah, Sovereign Lord, . . . I do not know how to speak; I am only a child."[7]

He, too, has missed the point, although eventually, through the Lord's persistence, he responds. He does not at that moment have faith that God will provide for those he sends out.

The provision, as the Bible makes clear, is often a thoroughly supernatural one involving miraculous manifestations of the presence of God. The New Testament refers to them as "spiritual gifts." And this was the provision that so startled those moving into the current renewal. Except for a relatively small number of Pentecostals, few Christians had any understanding of, let alone faith in, the spiritual gifts. But as they responded to the Lord's call and his commission, they quickly found themselves empowered beyond their imaginations.

In many cases, possibly in most, the experience of power preceded any intellectual understanding of it, as with my first taste of prophecy in Mount Vernon. The people merely asked the Lord to baptize them in the Holy Spirit, and they charged ahead, praying in tongues, prophesying, praying for the sick, expecting miracles. Sooner or later, they got around to finding that the Scripture explained their experiences and also called for them to increase in understanding and maturity.

This pattern caused many evangelicals and others to criticize the so-called charismatics for being experience-oriented and not well-grounded in Scripture. But the charge was often false in the long run, for the charismatics generally proved to be the most faithful to Scripture of any Christians. They merely had first found out that Christianity was indeed a new life and had a character that caused things to happen. It produced experiences. And those experiences did not always depend on knowledge, but always on grace.

Nonetheless, the genuine experiences were supported by the Bible. Even the excesses and abuses were explained.

St. Paul's first letter to the Corinthians was especially important in the early days of understanding—so important, in fact, that it was almost dangerously mistaken as "the charismatic gospel." It came close to getting undue emphasis for a short time. But, still, that was understandable; relatively little instruction was being provided through conventional channels.

But understanding and balance usually prevailed eventually, essentially because God was the source of the renewal and he was protective. It must always be remembered that even at their rowdiest the Pentecostals and the charismatics were certain of two things: Jesus was the Lord, and they were dependent on him. He honored that simple trust and eventually got them on track, even when they shot off on some tangent. And there were many tangents, usually an unwarranted emphasis on some particular passage of Scripture or some special doctrine or a spectacular spiritual gift. There were times of undue stress on deliverance or exorcism, shepherding and submission, baptism and rebaptism by immersion, and concern with timetables for the end times.

But the Spirit of truth and unity has had the last word in most cases, correcting and overruling mistakes and ultimately meeting faith with light. The process is still going on.

*　*　*　*

This pattern is the one found in First Corinthians. Ignorance and excess were corrected, and power was released. Chapters twelve, thirteen, and fourteen were especially important in this regard.

Immediately in this passage, the English-speaking reader runs into a word that caused widespread misunderstanding in the renewal, and still does from time to time. That word is "gifts." The reader of the King James Version and one or two other translations notices that the word is italicized, which means that it was not in the Greek text but was added to the English translation for clarification.

Unfortunately, for many readers, this muddies the

understanding and directs attention away from the
fact that *the gift* is the Holy Spirit himself, not some
particular manifestation. They begin to think that God
somehow gives them only one aspect or manifestation
of himself. They speak in tongues once, for instance,
and they think tongues is *their* gift, whereas the Spirit
in his wholeness is their gift, as he is for every
Christian.

St. Peter made this plain in his sermon on the day of
Pentecost:

"Repent and be baptized, every one of you, in the
name of Jesus Christ so that your sins may be
forgiven. And you will receive the *gift of the Holy
Spirit.* The *promise* is for you and your children
and for all who are far off—for all whom the Lord
our God will call."[8]

The gift—the promise—is the Holy Spirit.

But the muddiness doesn't stop there. The word
"gift" conveys to many Christians the idea that the
tongue or the prophecy or the working of miracles is
somehow a gift to them, something that for some
reason God has chosen to give to *them.* And this,
naturally, poses the threat of pride or even covetous-
ness. Some begin to think they are something special,
completely forgetting Paul's words:

Now to each one the manifestation of the Spirit is
given for the common good.[9]

The "gift" or manifestation is obviously given to the
church, not to the individual through whom it comes.
As Paul explained:

All these [manifestations] are the work of one and
the same Spirit, and *he gives them* to each man, *just*

as he determines.[10]

God definitely does not give a gift of healing, say, once and for all and leave it to the individual to spread it around among the needy. No, God gives each gift, performs each manifestation, to the one in need, for the common good. It isn't as though the Holy Spirit somehow divides himself up and gives this person a bit and that person another bit. He gives *himself* to an individual Christian and then is able to express or manifest himself freely as he sees fit. If that individual is in a situation where a prophetic word is needed, it matters not whether he sees himself as one with a gift of prophecy if the Holy Spirit chooses to speak through him. He may be the only one there with enough faith at the moment to speak for the Lord.

It is not proper to nitpick over words like this, however. The translators obviously needed to do something for the sake of clarification and the closest they could come, they felt, was with the word "gift." Some teachers believe understanding would be improved if the word were rendered "manifestation," but there is an uneasy vagueness about that too—so "gift" it is, as long as it is understood that the Spirit really is the gift and that the manifestations or gifts are bestowed solely by the grace of God. For the Greek word underlying the renewal's use of the word "charismatic" is *charis*, which is the word for "grace." Those things which we call charismatic are, just like salvation itself, based entirely on the grace of God.

* * * *

For some time in the early days of the current renewal—or at least it was so with me and others I saw—there was a tendency to rush past three verses in chapter twelve of First Corinthians, mentioned earlier, that proved to be terribly important. We were so eager to get to the "goodies" below that we missed their impact:

> There are different kinds of gifts, but the same Spirit. There are different kinds of service, but the same Lord. There are different kinds of working, but the same God works all of them in all men.[11]

Besides carrying a nice Trinitarian touch—Spirit, Lord, God (Father)—the three verses address a subject that was late in coming to the forefront in the renewal. In fact, ignorance of it caused considerable harm in some parts of the church. The truth was that Christians didn't have to be exactly alike. They had to learn that Christ did not insist on—nor even desire—conformity and uniformity among his followers. They had to see that there could be unity, even strength, in diversity.

I remember that, early on, I expected others to sound like me when they prayed or spoke in tongues or witnessed. I know also that many who did not speak forcefully in tongues or raise their hands while praising God or invoke the name of Jesus at every tenth word were often considered suspect. Style became more important than content for this reason. We merely failed to grasp that there were different kinds of gifts or manifestations, and there were different kinds of work to be performed with those gifts, and there were different ways or styles of doing that work.

Differences are good and proper as long as the Spirit is the motivator. He does not want to violate our different personalities, our different temperaments, our different backgrounds. Those differences are useful to him. After all,

> We are God's workmanship, created in Christ Jesus to do good works, which God prepared in advance for us to do.[12]

In 1 Corinthians 12:7, quoted previously, there is an important small point supporting a truth I've noted before and which the church is only now beginning to grasp with any force: the fact that all Christians are called to minister. St. Paul said the manifestation of the Spirit is given to "each one." The Spirit, in other words, doesn't work only in some elite corps. He works in *all* of God's people.

And then Paul laid down a terse description of the manifestations of the Spirit, although there is no reason to believe that he intended to enumerate here *every* aspect of the working of the third member of the Trinity. He seemed to be talking about the workaday sort of gift, the kind that should be expected in regular church meetings, for example. These weren't special ministries; he talked about those in other places. These were the kinds of activity the people of God were to expect—even desire[13]—when they gathered.

> To one there is given through the Spirit the message of wisdom, to another the message of knowledge by means of the same Spirit, to another faith by the same Spirit, to another gifts of healing by that one Spirit, to another miraculous powers, to another prophecy, to another the ability to distinguish between spirits, to another the ability to speak in different kinds of tongues, and to still another the interpretation of tongues. All these

are the work of one and the same Spirit, and he gives them to each man, just as he determines.[14]

One of nine gifts or manifestations mentioned here by St. Paul, all but two appear to fall into the "word" category. The remaining two, gifts of healing and miraculous powers, might be called the "miraculous" or physical type. Among the former, there is considerable overlapping and in practice a distinction is often difficult (and unimportant). And, of course, healing is definitely a miracle, the more obviously so when it is instantaneous, so even in the physical manifestations there is overlapping.

This is not the place for an exhaustive study of the spiritual gifts experienced by thousands in the charismatic renewal, but it might be helpful at least to provide a cursory look at the way they have usually been worked out.

The Message (or Word) of Wisdom

This manifestation, closely related to prophecy, has occurred openly before whole groups and privately between individuals. It often involves extraordinary and supernatural insight into seemingly impossible situations, providing a way where there appeared to be no way. It flows out of deep comprehension of the mighty acts of God and how they apply to the plight of an individual or group.

Just as the phrase, "message of wisdom," implies, it is the receipt of wisdom—often a sense of direction—that goes beyond what the minister would know in his natural, trained self. And it drives to the core of a need, providing light and understanding that move toward meeting that need.

The Message (or Word) of Knowledge

Closely related to the message of wisdom, as well as to prophecy, this gift provides what Paul's words imply—extraordinary knowledge or information that the minister would not have naturally. It often consists of a fact or facts about a person in need—his past perhaps, the cause of his need. It sometimes is knowledge about something or someone that the person involved has forgotten or repressed, information that needs to be brought forth and faced to allow healing to occur.

On the other hand, the knowledge may relate to something God has done rather than what the individual has done. This gift was evident in many ministries in recent years through which healing came. Kathryn Kuhlman, famous for a healing ministry, believed that the gift manifested through her was the word of knowledge about healings the Lord had performed in her meetings. She did not claim gifts of healing. Pat Robertson, the prominent Christian broadcasting executive and minister, who has become increasingly noted in recent years for the healings taking place when he ministers, likewise referred only to the word of knowledge being manifested through him. He laid no claim to any special healing gift. Both of these people, and many others through the years, seemed to receive an acute perception of when and how God was healing people as they themselves merely preached the Gospel.

Furthermore, it is common for the message of knowledge to be given in tandem with the message of wisdom. First will come the word of knowledge regarding a person or something God has done; then will come the word of wisdom about what to do with that knowledge. Many times the two manifestations are inseparable. God apparently refuses to be boxed into well-defined structures.

Faith

The black-and-white boundaries of the gifts are often blurred further when this manifestation flows right in on top of the messages of knowledge and wisdom. It consists of a startling surge of faith to believe what God has shown or done—faith that exceeds even the marvelous faith through which salvation comes. It is an ability, bestowed by grace, to believe and trust God in the face of any obstacle or any contrary circumstance.

The word of knowledge regarding healing is often accompanied by this supernatural faith. Perhaps a minister will speak forth that God is healing a tumor; then the recipient of the healing receives a tremendous certainty that it is indeed for him. And later examination proves that the two gifts have worked together. The tumor is gone.

Gifts of Healing

This manifestation of the Holy Spirit is simple, while at the same time so profound and mysterious as to defy grasp. It means just what it says: healing given through the prayers, the intercessions, of a human instrument chosen by God. And, like all the other gifts, it depends entirely upon the grace of God. Attempts to put formulas and techniques around it fail.

But the experience of the renewal is that oftentimes, the gift of healing is accompanied by the gift of faith and the word of knowledge, maybe working through more than one person, so that there is a positive awareness that the healing has been done. However, there are those times when the healing comes virtually as a surprise, when least expected. And it often comes to people who have little, if any, faith for it. It is this sort of grace—the totally unexpected—that often caused Miss Kuhlman to shake her head, shrug her shoulders, and smile almost wistfully. "I don't understand it," she said more than once. "It's sheer grace."

Miraculous Powers

This one, of course, sounds spooky. But it, too, is so profound as to be utterly simple. We have no choice but to look at it simply. The manifestation comes at those times when God, who is completely free, chooses to disrupt the natural order that he established, sustains, and controls, and causes something unnatural and supernatural to happen.

Jesus gave many examples when he was in bodily form. He stilled the wind and the waves, he walked on the water, he withered the fig tree, he passed through a vicious mob unscathed, he turned water into wine, he fed thousands of people with a few fishes and loaves on at least two occasions, he saw and knew Nathaniel when he was a great distance away. The Spirit of the Lord was truly upon him, this Word become flesh.

An interesting pattern was noticed in the renewal regarding this bestowal of miraculous powers. Christians by the thousands found that, immediately after being baptized in the Holy Spirit, they were extraordinarily expectant and confident that the Lord would in fact do what he had said he would do—meet all their needs. And in that great expectancy, that sort of brashness of faith, many little miracles seemed to occur around them as they went about their daily lives. They'd pick up a pickle jar and find the lid hopelessly stuck. Almost unconsciously they'd mutter, "Lord Jesus," and pop! the lid would almost fall into their hands. Or the car would start into a skid on a slick road. "O Lord," they'd mumble, almost under their breaths, and the car would straighten out magically.

But, unhappily, in many, many cases these miraculous little happenings seemed to dwindle in individual lives as the people continued in their walks. Thoughtful observers wrestled with this pattern and found that Spirit-filled Christians are still very human. And, being still in the world, they are touched by it, even if only slightly, and their childlike expectancy takes on an ever-so-thin crust.

Nonetheless, God continued to manifest himself occasionally in miraculous ways to meet needs according to his will, moving through a member or members of the body of Christ.

Prophecy

New Christians in the early stages of the renewal had some conceptual difficulty with this gift. Overemphasizing certain incidents from the Old Testament prophets in their attempts to learn, they quite understandably concluded that prophesying was foretelling, predicting the future. But steadily, under the prodding of St. Paul's insistence that they especially desire the gift of prophecy, they learned by experience that to prophesy is to speak forth what God wants said at a given time. It is speaking God's word into a situation. A cliché developed that says, "Prophecy is not foretelling, it is forthtelling," and as with most clichés it is true.

Many styles of prophecy are heard. Some people speak as though they have stepped right out of the

King James Version of the Bible. Some speak street language. Some are rather formal, "Thus saith the Lord," and some are conversational, "I think the Lord would have us know that. . . ." Some are definitely inspired, some are less so.

Prophecy, as the Scripture makes so clear, is a terribly important manifestation of the Spirit, and, with teaching and increasing commitment, members of the church have become more and more able to open themselves to the Lord, hear his word quite naturally and calmly through their Spirit-led thought processes, and then speak to the assembly with life-affecting results.

The Ability to Distinguish Between Spirits

Some confusion surrounding this manifestation arose at times as some, accustomed to the words of the King James Bible—"discerning of spirits"—were actually expecting a gift of general discernment, which really called for a gift of wisdom.

This particular manifestation came to be recognized as the divinely given perception of whether something or someone is motivated by good or evil, by God or Satan. It was a critically important gift from God during the early days of the Christian church, when there was no New Testament to measure things by. False prophets or teachers were discerned by the Holy Spirit's move upon a member of the body.

Of course, this work of the Spirit was extremely valuable in the charismatic renewal as the Lord moved his people into a new openness and freedom and there were many opportunities for false or misled teachers to lead the flock astray. Despite some painful moments, the Spirit protected the church.

Another aspect of this manifestation is found in the ministry to people beset by demons. The ministers have frequently found themselves able to recognize the type of demonic activity they are dealing with and thus to be more precise and effective.

The Ability to Speak in Different Kinds of Tongues

We arrive at the most controversial part of the renewal—speaking in tongues. This manifestation alone has wrought tremendous havoc during this century, and appeared to be more responsible than anything else for keeping evangelicals by the thousands from even breathing the word "charismatic." And the charismatics, of course, were not without blame in the alienation.

Terrible misunderstanding pervaded Christendom, both within and outside of the renewal. Some insisted that, unless one spoke in tongues, he had not been baptized in the Holy Spirit. Some insisted that tongues had been for another age and were now an instrument of Satan. Some cried, "It's emotionalism!" Some declared, "If you haven't spoken in tongues, you haven't been saved!"

But gradually the Scripture, practical experience, and common sense caused much of the bristling to subside, and more and more leaders accepted speaking in tongues as a legitimate Christian practice, even today. And it appears that a consensus has grown around an understanding that a Spirit-filled, Spirit-anointed believer does not *have* to speak in tongues, although large numbers maintain that such a believer *can* speak in tongues if he desires and that, furthermore, he probably will someday.

Many thousands have found that as they fully yield

themselves to the Lord and ask him to baptize them in the Spirit they immediately or soon afterward begin to speak in sounds, syllables, and words that are not from their own knowledge of language. They describe it as a "heavenly language" or a "language of praise," which they say enables them to praise and delight in the Lord in a new dimension.

Probably the most difficult part of speaking in tongues for most people has been grasping the idea that *they* are to do the speaking, even though the content is up to God. Most have the idea, at least for a while, that "if God wants me to speak in tongues, he's going to have to do it." From there they figure that the Lord will somehow "zap" them and cause them to speak involuntarily. And, of course, God doesn't do that, and many people wait a long time before finally getting the idea. They are to speak, and God is to give the utterance. By faith they are going to have to accept that what they say is not gibberish. It isn't long before they *know* they are not speaking gibberish.

Also complicating the renewal's understanding has been the fact that there are two categories of tongues-speaking. One is purely personal, between the believer and God, in which the language is not meant for other ears. The other is for the other members of the assembly and is audible. A majority understand the latter, when coupled with the interpretation of the tongue, to be tantamount to prophecy—a speaking forth on behalf of God. This, to me, appears to be St. Paul's teaching:

> He who prophesies is greater than one who speaks in tongues, unless he interprets, so that the church may be edified.[15]

However, there is a minority of knowledgeable Christians who believe that speaking in tongues is not a message from God, but rather prayer. They base this on St. Paul's words:

For anyone who speaks in a tongue does not speak to men but to God. Indeed, no one understands him; he utters mysteries with his spirit. . . . He who speaks in a tongue edifies himself.[16]

The construction of the passage and the context, however, seem to make it clear that this is only true for speaking in tongues that are *not* interpreted.

The Interpretation of Tongues
This manifestation, of course, goes hand in glove with speaking in tongues. It simply is the speaking forth in the language of the people that which has been spoken in the unknown tongue. As has been noted, it is generally believed to work with tongues to produce the equivalent of prophecy. When no one present is being inspired with the interpretation, then it is expected that those speaking in tongues will speak only to themselves and God. They are not to disrupt the other worshipers.[17]

Often, however, since people do not always know at first whether an interpretation will be given to someone else, a person might speak in tongues, pause, and then ask the Lord to give him the interpretation, which in most instances is granted, although it may not always be the perfect way.

* * * *

Since so much of the working of God with his people has through the centuries hinged on his Word—with the Word in one form or another always preceding

77

action—it is not strange that such a large proportion of his spiritual manifestations should come in word form. And it really doesn't seem strange that there is considerable overlapping among those word gifts. They are all like prophecy, in some degree, and require much the same understanding, attitude, and approach.

In the current renewal, that understanding, attitude, and approach eventually got onto good scriptural tracks in most circles, although many church leaders remained convinced that much more genuine prophecy was needed and that the church generally was severely lacking in power and direction because of this need. Their concern was understandable, because the Scripture makes it plain that the church must have prophetic voices; it must be edified in these destructive times, for the voices of destruction can only be expected to increase.

Those desiring the so-called word gifts, particularly prophecy, have found their best instruction in the book of Jeremiah. And, as is so often the case in the Scripture, the positive instruction comes intertwined in negative, harsh criticism of the false prophets of Jeremiah's time, forcing us to read between the lines. All of chapter twenty-three is informative, although scary, but the most pointed instruction begins midway:

> This is what the Lord Almighty says:
> "Do not listen to what the prophets are
>   prophesying to you;
>   they fill you with false hopes.
> They speak visions *from their own minds,*
>   *not from the mouth of the Lord.*"[18]

It couldn't be said more plainly. Prophecy is not

some man or woman's ideas; it is not mere human advice. It is to come "from the mouth of the Lord." The prophet is to hear it from the Lord.

But how? We read further:

> But which of them has *stood in the council of the
> Lord
> to see or to hear his word?*
> Who has listened and heard his word?[19]

What does *standing in the council of the Lord* mean? It obviously means spending time with the Lord; it obviously means praying, thinking about him, thinking with him, asking questions, listening with the inner man for answers.

The use of the word "council" in this prophecy is curious. Older translations rendered the word "counsel," but newer ones have turned to "council," seeming to follow more closely the Hebrew meaning of "session" or "company of persons in close deliberation," with overtones of intimacy and privacy. Was the Lord referring to the Trinity when he spoke, or was he talking of settings like those described in chapters four and five of the Revelation?

Experiences of twentieth-century prophets included both possibilities, but probably the most frequent experience was that of being in the presence of God, with Jesus or the Father as the central figure as revealed in the inner man by the Holy Spirit. However, significant numbers of God's people from time to time experienced within themselves the kind of images found in the Revelation, including vast numbers of beings and colors and sounds. Probably the most common experience in recent times was merely an intense awareness of the presence of God—Father,

Son, and Holy Spirit all at once—without any particular vision.

Jeremiah gave us a yardstick, however, to measure in a general way whether the prophet has truly stood in the council of the Lord:

> But if they had stood in my council,
>> they would have proclaimed my words to my people
>
> and would have turned them from their evil ways
>> and from their evil deeds.[20]

Here we see what the result of prophecy should be. False prophecy keeps the people in their evil ways; true prophecy works in the opposite direction.

However, we had words from the New Testament that must be laid in on top of Jeremiah's words lest the modern prophet lose his balance and fall to the other extreme. It has been hard for those in the renewal to remember that an important dimension has been added to the life of God's people since the sending of the Holy Spirit in a special way at Pentecost. The Spirit is at work upon them in a way that was not provided for in Old Testament times. This affects the prophet's approach. His purpose is to speak in such a way as to cause the people to allow the Spirit to work God's will in their midst.

That is why St. Paul was inspired to write:

> But everyone who prohesies speaks to men for their *strengthening, encouragement and comfort.*[21]

Prophecy works toward building up, not destroying. That is not to deny those times when it is necessary to do some cleaning up in order to build up, or to lance a festering sore to allow air and light to get at it. But prophecy, according to St. Paul, strengthens and encourages and comforts. It produces lightness, not heaviness and gloom, not despair, at least ultimately.

Unfortunately, in many parts of the renewal, words were spoken frequently in the name of the Lord that produced no edification. They only sank the suffering people lower. There was no light, no brightness. The Gospel seemed to become bad news.

But, at the same time, there was a tendency among some to speak only words like Pollyanna's—words that merely helped the suffering to wallow in their sin and pain. There was no recognition that sometimes people must catch a glimpse of the bad news before the good news can penetrate.

Thus the renewal struggled with balance—with the only true way being found by "standing in the council of the Lord."

But on those numerous occasions when the prophets had spent their time alone with God, living, healing waters poured across the church and even out into the world, which in ignorance and unbelief was collapsing from thirst.

* * * *

As the renewal gained maturity, it became increasingly clear that these sort of *ad hoc* gifts or manifestations of the Spirit had a deeper, more meaningful place in the quickening church. From them would come more permanent ministries, or specialties, if you will—some referred to them as offices—from which the functioning body of Christ would take shape.

But first, there had to come an awareness that God, capable of moving very supernaturally with stunning blessings of the Holy Spirit, also desired to move quite naturally through his people, utilizing their seemingly natural talents, and their mental and physical gifts. It was a painful learning process for those who tended to downgrade, if not reject, anything smacking of the natural man or world. But, fortunately, God was not in a hurry. Time is his.

CHAPTER SIX

Talents

Conversations like this one were heard hundreds of times in the last fifteen years:

"That was a beautiful solo you sang for us this morning, Mary."

"Oh, that wasn't me; that was the Lord."

And then there was this kind:

"What are you doing home, Joe? I thought you were away at school?"

"Oh, I stopped all that. I'm going to serve the Lord full time now and I don't need all that education. Jesus will give me what I need."

There were many variations, of course, but they drove to the same point: a disregard, even contempt, for anything that wasn't entirely spiritual. Anything pertaining to the natural man was viewed as useless. Natural talents, like singing or painting or excelling in mathematics, seemed almost to be an embarrassment.

This tendency, while fully understandable, has been a problem in the renewal, just as undue emphasis in the other direction—upon material, physical things—has been a problem for the church in other places and times. We Christians have apparently not escaped the pendulum characteristic that is so obvious in other parts of society. We swing from one side to the other, striking a brief balance from time to time, and then yielding to the pull to one side or the other. Our flaw is that we overdo some quality and carry it to excess, then we overcompensate for it, and end up carrying the opposite to excess. We sometimes resemble yo-yos.

Most who came into the renewal in the sixties had their roots in materialism and adulation of the intellect, and the quite predictable pattern for us was to swing all the way to an excessive dependence on things wholly spiritual. We were too new, too unschooled, to comprehend that while flesh and blood will not inherit the kingdom of God, the time for the change from flesh and blood in the twinkling of an eye to an imperishable being[1] has not yet come and we are still God's human ambassadors in the world. We had trouble—and most of us still have it—in working out the fact that we have been left in the world by our Lord and yet we don't belong to it. That's hard.

Another thing most of us overlooked for a long time was that one of our favorite Bible verses had something important to say about the world:

For God so *loved the world* that he gave his one and only Son, that whoever believes in him shall not perish but have eternal life.[2]

We failed to see that God *loves* the world. It's his creation, and he loves it. True, it is fallen, and he hates that; he hates what we have done to it. It has in a sense broken his heart. But he loves it, so much so that he ransomed it with the suffering and death of his only begotten Son.

If God loves the world, should we hate it? The answer is similar to the cliché describing our mandated attitude toward people: "We should love the sinner, but hate the sin."

Furthermore, we had difficulty getting a handle on just who and what Jesus was during his incarnation. We hadn't digested the passages of Scripture that offer help in this, those teaching the very slippery lesson that Jesus was both God and man.

Your attitude should be the same as
that of Christ Jesus:
   Who, being *in very nature God*,
      did not consider equality with God
         something to be grasped,
   but made himself nothing,
      taking the *very nature of a servant*,
      being made in human likeness.
   And being found in appearance as a man,
      he humbled himself
      and became obedient to death—
         even death on a cross![3]

Again, it's hard—beyond our imaginations. But Jesus was not merely a spiritual being. He took a real body, real flesh and blood. His flesh tore; his blood flowed. He ate ordinary food; he loved the lilies of the field; he worked with tools and wood.

Can we deplore such natural things? No, we are both physical and spiritual beings—we are both material and immaterial creatures—and both states were given to us by God. That's what we tended to forget.

Being like pendulums, we tended to swing toward

some of the characteristics of the Gnostics of the first and second centuries. They were people who slipped into heresy that threatened the early church for many years, deploring everything material and visible as evil, going so far as to deny the real humanity of Jesus. Some envisioned two Gods, one Old Testament God who created this "evil" world and a second, higher God who was head of the "good" spiritual world. The early church fathers had their hands full maintaining the balance of the true faith. And so did some of the "fathers" of the charismatic renewal, people like Michael Harper of England, who warned powerfully against tendencies toward this heresy.

Many went through difficult periods because of misunderstanding in this area. They had to become ingrained with the knowledge that God, who knew us all before we were born, who called us into being, has given us our natural gifts as well as our spiritual ones and is concerned about our physical lives as well as our spiritual lives. And they had to come to see that everything about us—all our gifts—are ultimately for God. Any talents, any special traits of personality and temperament are just as much from him and for him as are any spiritual gifts.

For *we are God's workmanship*, created in Christ Jesus to do good works, which God prepared in advance for us to do.[4]

God has made, and is making, his people what they are, and for a purpose. By being "born again,"[5] they are now both his physical *and* his spiritual workmanship and they have both physical and spiritual works to do. He has prepared it all. Can we do less than delight in all aspects of what he has done? Can we say we don't want anything to do with the physical and the natural?

The renewal has been working its way through to proper answers on these questions and, as the Bible forewarned, it has not been easy.

I can remember agonizing nearly ten years ago over a decision I had to make regarding a change in my work. I spent hours on my knees, and I fasted, and I searched the Scripture. I talked to other Christians. God just didn't seem to be saying anything. I went back to my knees; I paced the floor. Why couldn't I hear the voice of the Lord?

Finally, David McCahon of Wellesley, Massachusetts, one of my wisest brothers in the Lord—a man of extraordinary patience and calm—said, with a twinkle in his eye, "Bob, why don't you just do what seems right and trust God?"

The fog lifted. I looked around, with a calmer eye, and there was only one path open anyway. And it seemed right. God, of course, had worked *naturally*. He had opened only one way. And I walked in it. But I had expected something much more dramatic than that; I had expected to hear the voice of God, loud and clear. Instead, when I once opened my eyes, I saw his hand.

*   *   *   *

The thing the people of the renewal had to perceive was that their natural gifts, their talents, had value but that value became like gold when they consciously and overtly submitted them back to the Lord. Those talents were to be anointed, renewed, empowered, for his service.

We see something of this in the letter to the Romans:

Therefore, I urge you, brothers, in view of God's mercy, to offer your *bodies* as living sacrifices, holy and pleasing to God—which is your *spiritual* worship. Do not conform any longer to the pattern of this world, but *be transformed by the renewing of your mind*. Then you will be able to test and approve what God's will is—his good, pleasing and perfect will.[6]

Those bodies, those minds, those talents are not to be used the way they were before we yielded ourselves to the Lord, but they are far from useless. They are to be renewed with the power of the Spirit and then they will be able to do God's good, pleasing and perfect will.

What it all boils down to is that God has given us everything we have and consist of, and he wants it all back. He simply wants *us*—every bit of us. And he wants us to put every bit to work on those good works he has prepared beforehand. It sounds hard, but as we found out in the renewal, it really is easy, as Jesus said it would be:

Come to me, all you who are weary and burdened, and I will give you rest. Take my yoke upon you and learn from me, for I am gentle and humble in heart, and you will find rest for your souls. For *my yoke is easy and my burden is light*.[7]

It becomes easy and light because we are yoked to him and he carries the load; he takes us along the correct path. All that is required is the giving of self.

* * * *

Teachers like Terry Fullam shed additional light on this subject through their exposition of the Parable of the Talents. Jesus wasn't talking specifically about abilities and natural talents, but his words certainly applied. The talent of money he spoke of was a gift, just as the natural talent is.

In St. Matthew's account, Jesus is in the midst of several parables pointing toward his second coming. He is speaking of the kingdom of God:

"Again, it will be like a man going on a journey, who called his servants and entrusted his property to them. To one he gave five talents of money, to another two talents, and to another one talent, *each according to his ability*. Then he went on his journey. The man who had received the five talents went at once and put his money to work and gained five more. So also, the one with the two talents gained two more. But the man who had received the one talent went off, dug a hole in the ground and hid his master's money.

"After a long time the master of those servants returned and settled accounts with them. The man who had received the five talents brought the other five. 'Master,' he said, 'you entrusted me with five talents. See, I have gained five more.'

"His master replied, 'Well done, good and faithful servant! You have been faithful with a few things; I will put you in charge of many things. Come and share your master's happiness!'

"The man with the two talents also came. 'Master,' he said, 'you entrusted me with two talents; see, I have gained two more.'

"His master replied, 'Well done, good and faithful servant! You have been faithful with a few things; I will put you in charge of many things. Come and share your master's happiness!'

"Then the man who had received the one talent came. 'Master,' he said, 'I knew that you are a hard man, harvesting where you have not sown and gathering where you have not scattered seed. So *I was afraid* and went out and hid your talent in the ground. See, here is what belongs to you.'

"His master replied, 'You wicked, lazy servant! So you knew that I harvest where I have not sown and gather where I have not scattered seed? Well then, you should have put my money on deposit with the bankers, so that when I returned I would have it back with interest.

"'Take the talent from him and give it to the one who has the ten talents. For everyone who has will be given more, and he will have an abundance. Whoever does not have, even what he has will be taken from him. And throw that worthless servant outside, into the darkness, where there will be weeping and gnashing of teeth.' "[8]

It seems immediately clear that the Lord expects us to work with what he gives us; he expects it to multiply. After all, it belongs to him in its entirety anyway.

There are several parts to the lesson of the parable, although we must always remember that parables of the Lord were told to make a point, not to provide all the truth on everything. They must not be pressed beyond their application. One major point is that God gives to us and what he expects back from us is directly proportional to what he has given. He was pleased that the man doubled his five talents, but he gave the same commendation to the man who doubled his two talents. He didn't expect the man with the two to produce five. We can project that he would have commended the man with one similarly if he had doubled the one into two. God asks only proportionally to what he gives us. And, according to the parable, he gives us only according to what we can handle—"each according to his ability." He does not push us beyond our capacity.

It's interesting to note that the man who didn't use his talent failed to do so because he was afraid. He had an entirely wrong view of his master, which is the case with many Christians. He was afraid of him, and he was afraid of himself—afraid he would fail. He lacked the willingness to step out and use that which had been given to him. And there have been Christians like that in the renewal. They have been afraid to use their God-given natural talents. Some were afraid they'd fail, which revealed a low view of the power of the Lord to quicken those natural gifts for his service. Or else, they thought they might be too presumptuous or too showy if they stepped out and put their talents to work. They were afraid of criticism from God and their fellow Christians, which also suggests a pretty low opinion of God and his people.

To me, it seems safe to find in this parable a sense that it would be far better to take a chance with what the Lord gives us—even if we should lose it (which we won't)—than to do nothing. The Lord would rather have us fail than do nothing. This seems plain from the harshness of the punishment meted out to the lazy servant. People in the renewal had to come to see the perversion of God's goodness that was disclosed in laziness. Indeed, this is a matter of ongoing concern within the church.

To sum up the renewal's lesson from the parable: God gives us many natural gifts in the form of talents and abilities. We must not be afraid to use them if they are dedicated to him. In fact, to hold back is to fall short of what he expects—and that is sin.

* * * *

The Bible is full of good illustrations of God's anointing of talented people to make their talents more useful to his purpose. Moses is central to some of the examples.

In the book of Numbers, we see him struggling painfully with the difficult job of trying to lead the Israelites to the Promised Land. They were not an easy people to lead and they were certainly more than one person could handle. They were rebellious; they were complainers. They wandered away from God at the drop of a hat, and they were dissatisfied with his provision. Moses finally reached the end of his rope, crying out, in effect, "O God, why have you dumped all this on me?" But God had a plan:

> The Lord said to Moses: "Bring me seventy of Israel's elders *who are known to you as leaders and officials* among the people. Have them come to the Tent of Meeting, that they may stand there with you. I will come down and speak with you there, and I will take of the Spirit that is on you and *put the Spirit on them*. They will help you carry the burden of the people so that you will not have to carry it alone."[9]

It was Fullam who caused me to see something that was very plainly written. God had a task of great difficulty and importance to be done and he called forth some people to do it. But they weren't just any old seventy people. They were men of recognized ability; they had talents. They were already known as "leaders and officials." But God then took those talents and anointed them with the Spirit to enable them to do the task he had called them to. The talents were important and useful, but they required the anointing of the Spirit to make them useful to God's purpose.

Moses provided another example, as found in the book of Exodus, both in chapters thirty-one and thirty-five. He was being given specific instructions on the construction of the Tabernacle, work far more difficult and demanding than he or any ordinary person could hope to accomplish. But, again, God had a plan:

> Then Moses said to the Israelites, "See, the Lord has chosen Bezalel son of Uri, the son of Hur, of the tribe of Judah, and *he has filled him with the Spirit of God, with skill, ability and knowledge* in all kinds of crafts. . . . And *he has given* both him and Oholiab son of Ahisamach, of the tribe of Dan, *the ability* to teach others. He has *filled them with skill* to do all kinds of work . . . So Bezalel, Oholiab and every skilled person *to whom the Lord has given skill and ability* to know how to carry out all the work of constructing the sanctuary are to do the work just as the Lord has commanded."[10]

This passage offered great enlightenment because it was immediately apparent that God had given those men both the Spirit and their natural ability. Obviously he had prepared them for that job. They were not merely two guys off the street. They were people of skill, and that skill was anointed by the Spirit to consummate its usefulness.

Samson provided another illustration. This man, gifted by God with rare strength and physical ability, also required the anointing of the Holy Spirit:

> Then the Spirit of the Lord came upon him in power. He went down to Ashkelon, struck down thirty of their men, stripped them of their belongings and gave their clothes to those who had explained the riddle.[11]

In the New Testament, Jesus is the classic illustration. He was the Son of God, a person without sin, gifted with insight and wisdom from childhood. He had talent and ability. But he, too, this divine being who deigned to become man, received the anointing of the Spirit, according to the Gospel accounts, to do the tasks appointed him by his Father. St. Luke recorded it this way:

> When all the people were being baptized, Jesus was baptized too. And as he was praying, heaven was opened and *the Holy Spirit descended on him* in bodily form like a dove. And a voice came from heaven: "You are my Son, whom I love; with you I am well pleased."[12]

The rest of the chapter is taken up with the genealogy of Jesus through his supposed father, Joseph, and then chapter four opens with these words:

> Jesus, *full of the Holy Spirit*, returned from the Jordan and *was led by the Spirit* in the desert.[13]

A bit further along, we read:

> Jesus returned to Galilee *in the power of the Spirit*.[14]

And from there, we find the Lord going about to preach the good news to the poor, to heal the sick, to cast out demons—to fulfill his appointed ministry on earth, utilizing thirty years worth of learning, growth, and maturity under the anointing of the Holy Spirit.

Thus many people of the charismatic renewal have found themselves nodding their heads as the light of understanding has gone on and muttering, "If this was right for the Lord, can we do anything less?"

* * * *

In the sixties and seventies, there were many specific

examples of the anointing of talents and their multiplication among ordinary people in the renewal.

I knew pastors and priests who had come from excellent backgrounds and solid educational experiences, men definitely gifted in such natural ways that they and their friends often forgot that the gifts had come from God, and yet their ministries were rather weak. Their callings, so promising in the beginning, just did not seem to be reaching fulfillment. And then they were touched by the Holy Spirit and brought into the fullness of God. Their talents, their personalities, and the fruit of their training, were clothed with power from on high and their ministries blossomed, not always in terms of great numbers but always in terms of power and quality.

Dennis Bennett was a notable example of this, stepping forth into a ministry that was to have unprecedented impact on the Episcopal Church and other denominations as well. Jim Brown of the Presbyterian Church was much the same, and the examples within the Roman Catholic Church were endless. The same was true of many independent churchmen. Even those who had been reared in the Pentecostal denominations but who had grown stale found new bursts of power and achievement as God moved all across the Christian board.

But more than pastors and priests were involved. In music and the arts particularly were there great creative explosions under the inspiration of God's Spirit. Songwriters gave their talents to the Lord and marvelous music began to be heard. Singers did the same and found a quality and expression that was new. Writers, too, men and women trained in journalism and creative writing, schooled in philosophy and history, entered into new levels of written communication. And Christian athletes found a dimension of performance they had never dreamed of, as long as they stayed in God's will.

In Westchester County, New York, I knew a scientist for a major corporation whose professional work was thought to have no particular role in God's purpose. Science was merely his field for earning a livelihood, like St. Paul's tent making; the ministry came at other times. But that thinking was faulty in this case. God had a purpose in the man's laser research and quickened his talents so that just at the right moment, when his work had bogged down and the project was in jeopardy, he intervened by the Holy Spirit. Utilizing the scientist's skill and experience on the project to that date, he caused him to make a move that, as though by accident, locked the laser beam in and brought the work to a successful conclusion. The man's professional standing was enhanced and his witness for Christ surged ahead.

One of the most dramatic cases of God's anointing of a Christian's talents, training, and background for his special purpose came in the life of Pat Robertson, president of the Christian Broadcasting Network, one of the world's powerful instruments of Christian outreach. Robertson was the son of a United States Senator, well educated in secondary school and college, trained as an officer in the Marine Corps, graduated from Yale Law School, and rising in the structure of one of America's biggest corporations. He was handsome, charming, and married to a smart and pretty woman.

And then God, who had been working in his life without his knowing it, began to move more overtly, and

Robertson became a committed Christian. Events moved quickly, and he soon was baptized in the Holy Spirit. His multiple talents and advantages were brought under the power of the Holy Spirit, he went to seminary for schooling in things Christian, and he waited for God's direction. It came rather startlingly, and he was directed to go to the Tidewater area of Virginia, with seventy dollars to his name, to establish a Christian television station.

That was in the early sixties. Today that feeble little operation has grown into a network of four major TV stations, six radio stations, and a hundred and fifty affiliate TV stations carrying Christian programs literally around the world.

Robertson, like so many others, came to appreciate the fact that God could use his natural abilities, which had been given to him in the first place, as long as they were under the Lordship of Jesus Christ and the anointing of the Holy Spirit.

* * * *

Lest there be a misunderstanding, it should be pointed out that the charismatic renewal has not been just one big professional success story, although sometimes in our telling of the many dramatic testimonies that idea might be conveyed. No, the purpose of the anointing of the Holy Spirit is to accomplish God's will, to serve the Lord, not to provide fame and fortune for individuals, even though that occasionally occurs.

Probably the best way to describe it is that people have been enabled to accomplish significantly more that is meaningful in the Lord's eyes than they were able to do without the anointing of the Holy Spirit. They were, in fact, enabled to accomplish *all* that the Lord asked them to do, if they followed him in every step. Furthermore, they saw that *all* of God's gifts were good.

But, even after those lessons, there was a lot left to learn. Thousands, even millions, had undergone unbelievable experiences with God individually—vertically, so to speak. But that was to seem easy compared with the horizontal experiences. People, even Christians, are not always easy to get along with, let alone work with.

CHAPTER SEVEN

How to Grow Up

As a moviegoer, I always admired Gary Cooper. He was a man's man, or at least he was on the screen—gentle and kind, yet with an inner strength that came to the surface at just the right moments. Jimmy Stewart was a lot like that too. And, although I was always a little embarrassed about it in front of my more arty friends, I always liked John Wayne. These actors made rugged individualism real, right, and good. And millions of us who were reared in America were rugged individualists, at least in our own minds.

Herbert Hoover got credit for modern usage of the term "rugged individualism," although he disclaimed that credit. It was in a campaign speech in 1928, delivered in New York, that he referred to "the American system of rugged individualism." Later, in a book, *The Challenge to Liberty*, published in 1934, he wrote the following paragraph. It is significant to my thoughts on Cooper, Stewart, and Wayne:

> While I can make no claim for having introduced the term 'rugged individualism,' I should be proud to have invented it. It has been used by American leaders for over a half-century in eulogy of those

God-fearing men and women of honesty whose stamina and character and fearless assertion of rights led them to make their own way in life.

They are noble words, and many Americans have that kind of nobility ingrained in them. Especially is this true of millions of Christian believers. And yet, paradoxically, such idealism has been behind one of the most difficult adjustments in attitude that Christians responding to God's call in the twentieth century have had to make. Our true and correct love of democracy, our ingrained rugged individualism, has made it extremely difficult for us to see, deep down inside ourselves, that in matters of the church we are dependent on other people. *Dependent.* That is a hard word for a rugged individualist.

I heard this best explained by Terry Fullam a few years ago:

> I am a firm believer in democracy. It is the American way, and I believe no better way of governing a nation has been put forth. After all, it seems to me, two hundred million people more or less going at cross purposes can do far less damage than one or two with absolute power.

But, as he and others have said, the church of Jesus Christ is not a political nation, and it is not a democracy. It is a body of people with a King, a Lord, a Head. The members of that body are absolutely dependent upon their Head and—this is often the hard part—upon one another. They cannot be rugged individualists in their relationships with one another. (But they can still like Gary Cooper.)

* * * *

It would appear that the church has rarely grasped

and sustained the notion that Jesus is putting together a kingdom that, for this present age and for purposes of understanding by mere mortals, can only be described as a human body. For the church *is* a real body—a living, dynamic, growing organism. Christians have nodded their heads at the words, thinking of them as theological or mystical or metaphoric, but rarely since the first century have they in any large-scale way acted like a real body with real members, with only one of them—Christ—as the Head. And yet, that was the word given to the church by St. Paul at the outset:

> The body is a unit, though it is made up of many parts; and though all its parts are many, they form one body. So it is with Christ.[1]

From the beginning there has been only one body, and there is still only one body. Christ is building only one church. It is a unit, made up of many individual and very differing parts. And to nail the point down more tightly, St. Paul added this:

> Now you *are* the body of Christ, and each one of you is a part of it.[2]

There are times to be very literal with the Scripture, and this is one of those times. Paul could have said, "You are *like* a body," but he, a precise man, said, "You *are* the body." And that's where we've missed it.

Fortunately, however, the winds of renewal are blowing away the fog, and we're seeing the truth, even if we are having a bit of trouble working it out.

The second half of chapter twelve of First Corinthians has been helpful. First, St. Paul showed us that we were brought into the body by the Spirit:

> For we were all baptized by one Spirit *into* one body.[3]

The church is not a club that we join by signing up and paying dues. It takes an act of God to get us in. And, secondly, it is that same Spirit who keeps us, sustains us, in the body, according to the second half of that verse:

. . . and we were all given the one Spirit to drink.

Having thus drunk, and continuing to drink, of the same Spirit, we have power for unity if we desire it, according to a passage in another of St. Paul's letters:

Make every effort to keep the unity of the Spirit through the bond of peace. There is one body and one Spirit.[4]

Directing this body, this work of the Spirit, St. Paul showed in several places, is its Head, Jesus. First:

And he is the head of the body, the church.[5]

Again:

And God placed all things under his feet and appointed him to be head over everything for the church, which is his body, the fullness of him who fills everything in every way.[6]

And again:

For the husband is the head of the wife as Christ is the head of the church, his body, of which he is the Savior.[7]

This was the most important lesson the church had to learn in the renewal. Jesus really *is* the Head of the church. St. Paul was not hypothesizing. And if the statement has any relevance whatsoever, it must mean that he can in fact function as the head. And that was the killer. Could he actually *run* the church? He said he would build it; could he run it too?

Those were hard lessons. And they still are; we don't have a perfect handle on the matter yet. But that's where the heart of the renewal lies. Jesus can build his church, which consists of many diverse members, and he can bring it to unity. Only he can. Input from his people is confined pretty much to willingness and patience.

* * * *

After the renewal faced the facts that the church is a body and that Jesus is the Head of that body, there was still the problem of understanding how he directed the body. Again, the best guidance turned up in Paul's first letter to the Corinthians:

However, as it is written:
  "No eye has seen,
    no ear has heard,
  no mind has conceived
    what God has prepared for
      those who love him"—
but God has revealed it to us by his Spirit.

The Spirit searches all things, even the deep things of God. For who among men knows the thoughts of a man except the man's spirit within him? In the same way *no one knows the thoughts of God except the Spirit of God.* We have not received the spirit of the world but the Spirit who is from God, *that we may understand what God has freely given us.* This is what we speak, not in words taught us by human wisdom but in *words taught by the Spirit,* expressing spiritual truths in spiritual words. The man without the Spirit does not accept the things that come from the Spirit of God, for

they are foolishness to him, and he cannot understand them, because they are spiritually discerned. The spiritual man makes judgments about all things, but he himself is not subject to any man's judgment:
"For who has known the mind of
  the Lord
that he may instruct him?"
But *we have the mind of Christ.*[8]

The Spirit, who has been given to God's people, searches the mind of God and reveals his will. I remember that the first time this manner of working penetrated my understanding, an image registered in my mind. It was a good one, although not to be pressed too far. Here I was on earth and there God was in heaven, and a flow, a stream, of water was coming down and washing through me and going back up into heaven and washing through God and coming back down to me. It was a steady, clear flow, passing through God and then through me, endlessly, depositing the things of God within me, flowing and washing, flowing and washing. I'm sure the Lord's reference to living water contributed to the image.

The thought doesn't hold up if carried too far, but it is as though the Holy Spirit is the "working arm" of God on earth, and one of his functions is to provide communication between heaven and earth, and vice versa. He simply takes the thoughts of the Lord and puts them into our thoughts. It is not spooky, or weird, working quite naturally and sensibly, although it results in one of the most remarkable truths imaginable: We have the mind of Christ!

A classic example of the naturalness of this communication is found in chapter fifteen of the book of Acts. The first church council, or at least the first one we know about, the Council at Jerusalem, had been held to decide the extent to which Gentiles who became Christians should be expected to follow the customs of Judaism. After hearing Barnabas and Silas tell of the miraculous things God was doing among the Gentiles, the council, led by James, concluded that "we should not make it difficult for the Gentiles turning to the Lord." Instead the council instructed the Christians to abstain from food polluted by idols, from sexual immorality, from the meat of strangled animals and from blood.

Then James gave a clue as to how this gathering of people had arrived at a consensus. In a letter to the Gentiles in Antioch, Syria, and Cilicia, he explained:

It seemed good *to the Holy Spirit and to us.*[9]

The Spirit, it seems, had spoken—perhaps by prophecy, perhaps only in their thoughts as they debated and reached a consensus—and they had agreed. Apparently it was quite simple and quite ordinary, but they knew they had received the thoughts of God and, seeming to operate with free will, they concurred, the implication being that they could have disagreed.

One gets the idea that pretty much the same thing happened at Antioch to launch the missionary travels of Paul. Luke tells us this in Acts:

In the church at Antioch there were prophets and teachers: Barnabas, Simeon called Niger, Lucius of Cyrene, Manaen (who had been brought up with Herod the tetrarch) and Saul. While they were worshiping the Lord and fasting, the Holy Spirit said, "Set apart for me Barnabas and Saul for the work to which I have called them." So after they had fasted and prayed, they placed their hands on them and sent them off.[10]

Again, God communicated his thoughts by the Holy Spirit—presumably in a prophetic utterance, perhaps merely conversationally—and the body obeyed the Head. Unity is implied.

From these examples, the Christians in the current renewal found that, besides grace, the main ingredients needed to live under the direction of the Head of the church were willingness and patience. We *have* the mind of Christ; all we have to do is *live as though we have it*, waiting for him to bring us into unity before we act. God, even within himself, operates on the principle of unity.

This means recognizing that all Christians are members of the body of Christ with a function within that body. It means recognizing that each one of them is led by the Spirit and will hear from the Lord if he is faithful. It means recognizing that the hand is not effective without the arm, that the mouth can move around only by the work of the legs and the feet, which demands unity. It means finding our place in the body and functioning there, because as St. Paul said:

. . . God has arranged the parts in the body, every one of them, *just as he wanted them to be.*[11]

We don't decide what our function is; God does. And St. Paul lectured hard to show that it is wrong to be too modest and say that because you're not a hand or an eye or some prominent, up-front member you do not belong to the body, just as it is wrong to be so proud and vain as to say that you don't need the lesser parts of the body since you are so prominent and important.[12] He was extraordinarily perceptive because so many people in the renewal have fallen into one of those two categories. They were either too shy or too pushy. "I can't stand up in front of people and speak the way he can; I just can't do *anything*," some said. Others thought, "God has given me everything needed to get this job done; I don't want a bunch of other people getting in the way." Meanwhile, the word to all was: Be what you are—a much-needed member of the body; don't try to be something else.

* * * *

There was a strong word that didn't register meaningfully with some of us merely from reading or hearing. We had to have it driven home by experience, which is the only way the lessons of Scripture can really be grasped by us in the long run. It was another teaching in First Corinthians:

> . . . those parts of the body that seem to be weaker are indispensable, and the parts that we think are less honorable we treat with special honor. And the parts that are unpresentable are treated with special modesty, while our presentable parts need no special treatment. But God has combined the members of the body and has given greater honor to the parts that lacked it, so that there should be no division in the body, but that its parts should have equal concern for each other.[13]

I was in Connecticut in the early seventies when that lesson flashed before me in real life. I was speaking at a luncheon of Christian women of all ages and backgrounds, although a sizable percentage of them lived in at least average affluence. I was an editor at *The New York Times* then and thus something of an oddity. Not many newsmen were professing faith in Christ in the early seventies (or in the late seventies, for that matter). And the restaurant meeting room was filled, probably with a hundred and fifty women.

I don't remember what I spoke about—but presumably it was something to do with the baptism in the Holy Spirit and presumably it was a successful talk. Many women stayed around afterward to shake my hand and to be prayed with. I was in the spotlight.

As the crowd thinned, and the time for my departure approached, I saw a woman moving toward me. I hadn't seen her before. She was rather short and fat, a bit swarthy; her hair was not well done. She was, in a word, unattractive. Something about her was distorted, it seemed, almost grotesque, and she limped. But a smile covered her homely face; it fairly burst forth, past uneven teeth and rough lips. She moved straight at me.

"Mr. Slosser! Hi!" She shoved a hand toward me. "I wanted to catch you before you left. I wasn't able to get up here while you were speaking."

I didn't know what to say, and I guess I smiled rather foolishly.

She went on. "I've been down with the little children. You know, baby-sitting."

My mind finished the unspoken fact: "So their mothers could be up here having fun and receiving ministry."

Looking back, I'm surprised I didn't fall down. For I was overwhelmed with a new realization. Swooning under the thralldom of the Spirit would have been understandable.

My thoughts went something like this: This twenty-five-year-old woman was deserving of far more honor than I, the star. She was the "weaker" part of the body of Christ that was indispensable, the part we think of as less honorable but which in truth is treated with more honor. This woman was lovely. God had given honor to the member who lacked it. I had been honored at the meeting. I had stood in the spotlight—probably even wallowed in it—and this woman, who was every bit as much a minister as I was, had remained out of sight, blessing people without recognition. Truly, she had received the greater honor—from God.

It was a magnificent lesson in the importance of the individual members of the body of Christ. I had a function at that noontime ministry to the Connecticut women, and so did that woman. I could not say to her, "I don't need you!" No, indeed. I hugged that woman as a sister, and I loved her. We were both members of the same family.

* * * *

It's good to note again that in the lesson I've just finished describing, I learned that I had a *function* within the body of Christ, and the baby-sitter had a function. We were both to be treated with honor. Furthermore, there was no sense of hierarchy between us. I, the teacher, the prophet, or whatever, was not to lord it over the one doing the more menial task. We were to function together as necessary members of the body, which had a Head, Jesus Christ. He was the Lord; neither of us was.

In the renewal, because we were very human, we had a lot of trouble with the matter of function. We tended to develop a hierarchy, which of course was the path the institutional church began slipping into 1,700 years ago. We lost sight of Christ's very plain words on this subject:

> Jesus called them together and said, "You know that those who are regarded as rulers of the Gentiles lord it over them, and their high officials exercise authority over them. *Not so with you.*

Instead, whoever wants to become great among you must be your servant, and whoever wants to be first must be slave of all."[14]

Not so with you. And yet we often tried to run our churches and assemblies like American corporations, with a chairman and a board of directors and other powerful officers. But Jesus said it was not to be like that. St. Paul showed us how God looks at Christ's body:

You are all sons of God through faith in Christ Jesus, for all of you who were baptized into Christ have been clothed with Christ. There is neither Jew nor Greek, slave nor free, male nor female, for you are all one in Christ Jesus.[15]

If God sees the body in that manner, can we do anything else?

But we struggled with it. There were ugly fights and quarrels, there was backbiting and name-calling. And many people were hurt. In the name of discipleship, tyranny and oppression reigned in many Christian groups. Some of the teaching was inaccurate; some of it was merely distorted and misapplied. Some leaders tried to run people's lives in ridiculous extremes. Inevitably, rebellion flared.

And Jesus had said, "Not so with you."

It appeared, as time went on, that the teachings of the Scripture were sinking in. The people more and more purposed to work with the whole Bible, not isolated parts of it, and to learn from mistakes. They began to see that the members of the body could function through the Spirit under the Head and that some functions frequently had a higher priority than others. And they struggled gamely with the principle that some members of the body had the ticklish function of guaranteeing that church life be carried on decently and in order:

> . . . everything should be done in a fitting and orderly way.[16]

It was not going to be easy to function with the authority that this sometimes required and not fall into rigid hierarchy. Only the Holy Spirit—from whom all the authority comes—could do it, working in *all* together.

* * * *

Probably the most life-changing instruction regarding the functioning of the body came from a relatively short passage in chapter four of St. Paul's letter to the Ephesians.[17] It is still the centerpiece of much teaching around the country.

> But to each one of us grace has been given as Christ apportioned it. This is why it says:
> "When he ascended on high,
>   he led captives in his train
>   and *gave gifts to men.*"

That seems obvious. Christ gave gifts to men. But there is a nuance here that we had to pick up. A later verse helped:

> It was *he who gave some* to be apostles, *some* to be prophets, *some* to be evangelists, and *some* to be pastors and teachers. . . .

The gifts he gave, then, were other people. The gifts were apostles, prophets, evangelists, pastors, and teachers. The next verse helped make it clear that the gifts were to the church, to God's people:

> . . . to prepare God's people for works of service. . . .

The gifts were given to God's people to prepare them for works of service, or for *the work of ministry*, as other translations rendered it. Christ gave gifts, which were certain ministries, to the church *so the church could then minister*.

Therein was one of the biggest lessons of all. The renewal still hasn't mastered it. The church—which is the body, the saints, the people, *all* the people—is to do the ministry. It is not for one man, or a group of men and women. It is for the church. All Christians are to minister.

And then there is the inevitable, "But why?" And the second half of the sentence says plainly why:

. . . so that the body of Christ may be built up. . . .

That is the way—and the only way—the body is going to be built up, both numerically and qualitatively. The church is being prepared to minister so that it, the church, can be built up.

The plan, according to this passage, is for Christ to give a comparatively small number of ministers to minister inside the body of Christ so the other members of the body can minister outside (and inside, too, as the body increases). It is to be a constant growing, maturing process, for the body of Christ is a living organism, not a stale institution.

Fullam spoke a strong word to the church about this process that had the ring of truth: "It seems to me that the Scripture clearly teaches that a Christian cannot come to maturity apart from the body." The next verse in the Ephesians passage appears to establish the point:

. . . until we *all* reach unity in the faith and in the knowledge of the Son of God and *become mature*, attaining to the whole measure of the fullness of Christ.

The passage concludes with phrases that create a yearning in the Christian's heart, a yearning to live in what God has prepared for his people:

> Then we will no longer be infants, tossed back and forth by the waves, and blown here and there by every wind of teaching and by the cunning and craftiness of men in their deceitful scheming. Instead, speaking the truth in love, we will in all things *grow up* into him who is the Head, that is, Christ. From him *the whole body*, joined and held together by every supporting ligament, grows and *builds itself up* in love, *as each part does its work.*

Yes, the renewal was sensing, as the seventies wound down, that this was the way the church had to go if the plea of Jesus for the unity of his church was to be fulfilled. It was sensing that no longer was a church to be dependent upon a priest or a pastor. The priest and pastor are merely members of the body. It was to be dependent upon its Head and then to utilize the gifts the Head was giving. There no longer was to be *one* minister. Everyone in the church was to minister, prepared by the several apostles, prophets, evangelists, pastors, and teachers the Lord provided. And, as one maturing body was fond of saying, they had to realize that in a sense the church exists for those who are not yet a part of it. They had to reach out into the world. That way the church would be built up.

* * * *

Another hard lesson for the renewal in this connection was recognizing that *Christ* gave the gifts to the church. It was not up to some leader to go around among the people and say, "Now, I think you'd make a good apostle," or "I believe you ought to try being a

113

prophet." Neither was it up to some eager individual to say, "I believe I'd make a good evangelist."

Such decisions were to be made by the Head of the church and he would communicate to his body by means of the Holy Spirit, which usually meant that the whole body was eventually told by him, or at least a significant part of it was. It usually worked out that about the time an individual was sensing that maybe God was calling him for a specific ministry, the rest of the body was beginning to perceive the same thing. It often required great patience. But everything fell into place and unmistakable strength was found in the accord of the body. The unity produced strength and safety—a fact that caused more and more churches to act on matters only after complete unity had been attained.

Fortunately, most people didn't bog down in their ministries with efforts to place strictly defined limits on them. They rarely stopped to think about whether they were functioning as an apostle or a prophet, an evangelist or a teacher. There was a lot of overlapping, but the functions were all performed in one way or another, and people just charged ahead with trying to build up the church.

Nonetheless, it was helpful to see what the Bible seemed to say about the ministries, just to make sure that the work the Lord intended was being carried out.

A pretty good understanding of the function of an apostle, for example, is found in the book of Acts during the account of the first church's choosing of seven men to handle the daily distribution of food. We find the apostles giving their own description of their function within the body:

So the Twelve [apostles] gathered all the disciples together and said, "It would not be right for us to neglect *the ministry of the word of God* in order to wait on tables. Brothers, choose seven men from among you who are known to be full of the Spirit and wisdom. We will turn this responsibility over to them and will give our attention to *prayer and the ministry of the word.*"[18]

They obviously considered themselves to be concerned primarily with the ministry of the word of God—the Scriptures certainly and, almost as certainly, the teachings of Jesus that had not then been committed to writing. In the first verses of the book of Acts, we see that Jesus appeared to them over a period of forty days, "giving instructions through the Holy Spirit to the apostles he had chosen." To them, these instructions would have been described as "the word of God." They would later be written down and eventually receive the status of Scripture.

We get a good indication of what this ministry of the word consisted of by looking at the Acts accounts of what the apostles proclaimed. In virtually all cases, it involved a statement of the facts of salvation history, often going back into Old Testament times and climaxing with the declaration that Jesus had been sent, crucified, and resurrected, and that he had ascended, been exalted, and poured out the Holy Spirit.

The picture is enlarged as we tie this in with a description of what the Christians did in that first church:

They devoted themselves to the apostles' teaching and to the fellowship, to the breaking of bread and to prayer.[19]

This is probably the best indication of the activity of the first church that we have, and the apostles obviously functioned as overseers of that activity, as proclaimers, as teachers, as "fathers." They had something of a guardian function apparently, especially in connection with the breaking of bread—the Lord's Supper. This was central to the early church's worship although it probably had not taken the form of a eucharistic celebration at that time, still falling within the framework of a common meal, to which the Lord Jesus was invited and expected to come. A common prayer was "*Maranatha*"—"Come, Lord Jesus."

While looking at this function of the apostle within the body, we cannot lose sight of the fact that the word "apostle" means "one who is sent out." The apostles moved about, and one of their functions, especially in those first days, was to establish churches, staying for indefinite periods, and then moving on. In the sense that all Christians are in one way or another "sent out" under the great commission of Christ, then they all have something of an apostolic function.

As for the function of prophets, it was touched on in the review of the gifts or the manifestations of the Spirit. They are the ones who stand in the council of the Lord and then speak for him, serving as his mouthpiece, as it were. And in the sense of Ephesians four, this is an ongoing ministry for some people, not a sometime thing. The prophet is a gift to the church for its upbuilding.

The Bible also offered guidance for those in the renewal seeking a more precise understanding of the function of an evangelist, although the name itself seemed to convey a full meaning—one who tells the good news. The label is used with the name of Philip in

Acts 21:8, who is presumably the same Philip who ministered to the Ethiopian eunuch as described in Acts 8:27-40. This Philip told the Ethiopian "the good news about Jesus," apparently bringing him to a decision, for he then baptized him. And that is the difference between an evangelist and the other proclaimers of the word: He seeks to bring his audience, whether one or a thousand, to a decision about Christ. He seeks to lead that audience, then and there, into the church. Fullam described the function aptly: "An evangelist is really a baby-doctor. He brings forth newborn babes in Christ."

And in the renewal, men and women were raised up specially prepared and anointed just for that ministry. They were irrepressible and irresistible in their presentation of the Gospel, and they were ready and eager to make that presentation at any time—on a street corner, on an airplane, at the back of the church after the service. They had the God-given knack for leading people to the Lord in raw, ungilded evangelism.

The function of a pastor was not as easy to nail down as the others. It required some searching of Scripture to determine that several words were used interchangeably to describe the same function. "Pastor" was used least of all, appearing in the New Testament only in the Ephesians four passage. But by studying the functions, one could see that these titles bore essentially the same meaning: bishop, overseer, presbyter, elder, shepherd, and pastor. A description of one fits the others.

Both St. Peter and St. Paul provided insight on this function. As shown in Acts, Paul met at Miletus with the elders from Ephesus and at one point said to them:

Guard yourselves and *all the flock* of which the Holy Spirit has made you *overseers.* Be *shepherds of the church of God,* which he bought with his own blood. I know that after I leave, savage wolves will come in among you and will not spare the flock. Even from your own number men will arise and distort the truth in order to draw away disciples after them. So *be on your guard!*[20]

They were to be shepherds; they were to care for the flock, feeding it, watching over it, protecting it from wolves. And it was noteworthy that these early churches had more than one elder or pastor. They didn't speak of just one elder of a church, but rather "the elders." St. Peter, meanwhile, said it this way:

To the elders among you, I appeal as a *fellow elder,* a witness of Christ's sufferings and one who also will share in the glory to be revealed: Be *shepherds of God's flock* that is under your care, serving as *overseers*—not because you must, but because you are willing, as God wants you to be; *not greedy* for money, but eager to *serve; not lording it over* those entrusted to you, but *being examples to* the flock.[21]

It is interesting that the apostle, who frequently ministered far and wide carrying out his apostolic function, also apparently served as an elder, perhaps in Rome where this letter is thought to have been written, or perhaps he referred to earlier days in Jerusalem. But he saw himself in both roles—as elder and apostle, the former being local, the latter, translocal.

His words are precise in revealing the attitude that should reign within anyone calling himself elder-shepherd-overseer. Most importantly, he must not lord it over the flock. He has a function; the members of the flock have other functions. They must all submit to one another out of reverence for Christ.[22]

The New Testament also provided the renewal unusual detail regarding the character that should be found in elders, bishops, and overseers. It was most prominent in St. Paul's letters to Timothy and the one to Titus. Here is an excerpt from the latter:

> An elder must be blameless, the husband of but one wife, a man whose children believe and are not open to the charge of being wild and disobedient. Since an overseer is entrusted with God's work, he must be blameless—not overbearing, not quick-tempered, not given to much wine, not violent, not pursuing dishonest gain. Rather he must be hospitable, one who loves what is good, who is self-controlled, upright, holy and disciplined. He must hold firmly to the trustworthy message as it has been taught, so that he can encourage others by sound doctrine and refute those who oppose it.[23]

As was so often the case, it was Fullam who called my attention to the very positive lesson about elders and shepherds that could be derived from a passage of negative criticism leveled by the prophet Ezekiel in behalf of the Lord:

> Woe to the shepherds of Israel who only take care of themselves! *Should not shepherds take care of the flock?* You eat the curds, clothe yourselves with the wool and slaughter the choice animals, but you do not take care of the flock. You have not *strengthened the weak* or *healed the sick* or *bound up the injured.* You have not *brought back the strays* or *searched for the lost.* You have *ruled them harshly and brutally.* So *they were scattered because there*

119

was no shepherd, and when they were scattered they became food for all the wild animals.[24]

Unhappily, and yet understandably, the elders, shepherds, bishops, overseers, and pastors of the church of Jesus Christ have not mastered this lesson, even under the blessings of the charismatic renewal. But there has been movement forward in many areas. Many congregations have seen that this function, which in so many ways calls for the same character and attitude that is demanded in all the ministries outlined by St. Paul in his letter to the Ephesians, can be carried out in these waning years of the twentieth century. I am convinced it *must* be carried out—even though it may be one of the most difficult hurdles—if we are to see the fulfillment of God's purpose.

We had little trouble, even from the beginning of the renewal, in understanding the function of a teacher in the body of Christ. But even though we thought we knew what the function was, we still didn't produce many strong teachers for a number of years. There were a handful of noted ones, but if we were reading St. Paul correctly, he was calling for each body, each church, to have teachers, probably more than one. And that was not the case.

St. Paul described himself to Timothy as a teacher, as well as a herald, or preacher, and an apostle. He said he was a teacher of the "true faith to the Gentiles."[25] As a teacher, in other words, his subject was "the true faith," meaning apparently the whole of the Gospel, the whole Christian life flowing out of that Gospel. In another word to Timothy, who was also a teacher as well as an overseer—"my true son in the faith"—he added this:

Do your best to present yourself to God as one approved, a workman who does not need to be ashamed and who *correctly handles the word of truth.*[26]

He elaborated a bit further on:

Don't have anything to do with foolish and stupid arguments, because you know they produce quarrels. And the Lord's servant *must not quarrel*; instead, he must be kind to everyone, able to teach, not resentful. Those who oppose him he must *gently instruct*, in the hope that God will grant them repentance leading them to a knowledge of the truth. . . .[27]

Moving on, he showed that the teacher's material was to be found in the Scriptures. They are "God-breathed" and "useful for teaching, rebuking, correcting and training in righteousness, so that the man of God may be thoroughly equipped for every good work."[28]

He also gave a clue about how teachers were to gather their material and be trained:

And the things you have heard me say in the presence of many witnesses entrust to reliable men who will also be qualified to teach others.[29]

Teachers, in summary, are to teach the true faith, as found in Scripture, carefully and gently, instructing others who will in turn instruct still others. The body of Christ is to be built up.

"For the lips of a priest ought to preserve knowledge, and from his mouth men should seek instruction—because he is the messenger of the Lord Almighty."[30]

Making this ministry extremely hard in the early stages of the renewal was the fact that so few of the institutional churchmen had been thoroughly grounded in the Scriptures. Their seminary work had not prepared them to teach others from the Bible, and they had to study hard to overcome the lag. As the seventies were drawing to a close, there was evidence of progress in this area, thanks in large part to the untiring efforts of the teachers God raised up early and to the marvels of tape recording, television, and radio. Many of the prominent teachers were concentrating their work among small, intense groups of leaders. They were teachers teaching teachers.

* * * *

As I said at the beginning of this chapter, perhaps the single most difficult aspect of trying to restore the Christian ministry to the power and the structures found on the pages of the New Testament has been the matter of individualism, the seemingly ingrown determination to maintain privacy in every part of life. And this determination ran counter to the sort of collaboration that Christians apparently are called to. The concept of the body mandated closeness, and many of us still wanted everything, even those we loved, held a little bit at arm's length.

Furthermore, the every-Christian-is-a-minister concept called for a willingness to step forward, out into the open occasionally, and to have the nerve—the audacity, in the world's eyes—to do something in the name of Jesus Christ, confident that the Holy Spirit would demonstrate his power as needed. Many of us thought that was presumptuous, and there were others of us who used that word but mainly feared failure.

And naturally there was a reluctance on the part of

some professional ministers to open the door to "amateurs" to share the work, even though they had more than they themselves could do. Furthermore, plurality of leadership sounded awkward. How would anything ever get done? Church people never agree on anything. But steadily there came a trust in many places that the Holy Spirit could produce a unity, if there was a determination and a willingness on the part of the people to achieve it.

And steadily, more and more apostles, prophets, evangelists, pastors, and teachers were seen in local churches, often doing outstanding work, sometimes stumbling, but maturing day by day. They weren't always called apostles, prophets, and teachers. They were just "Joe Blow, who really seems to have a knack for that," but they nonetheless *were* apostles and prophets—Christ's "gifts to men." And in the face of great obstacles, the body of Christ was being built up and it was more and more reaching "into all the world."

But, remarkably, the mastery of God's way to minister was not the final, or the toughest, lesson in clearing the clouds away from the Lord's call for complete unity in his church. No, there were—and still are in most places—bigger steps to be taken in this age of the Holy Spirit.

CHAPTER EIGHT

Together

Running through the steady learning and growth of the body of Christ in the charismatic renewal were several progressions that must not be minimized. They weren't sequential, but often moved together, sometimes merging, sometimes spinning off into little identifiable segments all their own.

First, it must be abundantly clear to anyone reviewing the last fifteen or twenty years that, contrary to criticisms often made in strongly evangelical or fundamentalist circles, the Christians in the renewal were deeply committed to, and relentlessly increasing in knowledge of, the Holy Scriptures. They were often unfairly accused of being solely experiential and lacking any foundation on which faith could stand.

Having been fortunate enough to move in and out of most parts of the Christian spectrum, from moderately liberal to ultraconservative in theology and biblical view, I found no Christians with a deeper respect for the Scripture than the so-called charismatics. As I said in the previous chapter, thoroughly equipped teachers were not always available, and that was a handicap at first, but the individuals themselves, as

125

they experienced more and more of the Spirit's love and power, were untiring in their personal study and reliance on the Scripture. They made mistakes, and they spun off on tangents. But as time went on, their attitude seemed to reflect Article VI of the thirty-nine Articles of Religion found in the *Book of Common Prayer:*

> Holy Scripture containeth all things necessary to salvation: so that whatsoever is not read therein, nor may be proved thereby, is not to be required of any man, that it should be believed as an article of the Faith, or be thought requisite or necessary to salvation. In the name of the Holy Scripture we do understand those canonical Books of the Old and New Testament, of whose authority was never any doubt in the Church.

I can remember the development of my own understanding of the worth and the place of the Bible. Before my conversion I perceived the Bible to be somehow "sacred," a bit scary perhaps, mysterious, and confusing. I had read parts of it in college in a literature course but I really knew very little about it—and cared very little about it for that matter. I never thought much about it, which is sort of the way I was about God and the possibilities of his existence before he began changing my life rather sharply.

At any rate, I was born again, baptized in the Spirit, and actually witnessing to the power of the Lord, and I still hadn't fully come to grips with the Bible. I read it, and certainly learned from it, but I wasn't necessarily convinced that it was the word of God, that it was indeed true throughout, given by God to his people.

As time went on, and I from time to time pondered

the matter of the inspiration of the Scripture, its total reliability, and so on, I found myself, ever so gradually, simply accepting the Bible as true. With hindsight I can see that the process went something like this: I was reading the Bible regularly, and studying it with other people. As I would grasp a principle or a promise, being very eager and gung-ho, I would put it to the test. And it never failed. I can almost hear myself saying, "Son of a gun, it works!" So I'd keep going, and pretty soon I'd grasp something else, try it, and see that it was true. After many months, I looked up one day and said to myself, "How can you doubt the truth of the Bible? Everything you've trusted in has proven correct." And from that point on, I simply accepted the Bible as the inspired word of God, his revelation to his people. I did acknowledge at that time, however, that although I believed it to be fully true, there were things about it I didn't fully comprehend. And I suppose that's the way it will be until I get to be with the Lord—although I do find those incomprehensible parts shrinking and shrinking as I more completely yield to the guidance of the Holy Spirit and experience the unity and completeness of the Scripture.

As for me, Cervantes said it best through Don Quixote's sidekick, Sancho: "The proof of the pudding is in the eating."

* * * *

Also extremely important to the renewal—indeed, a genuine milestone—was the virtually discarded experience of worship. Except for significant but relatively isolated little pockets, the church of Jesus Christ had allowed the concept of true worship of the Creator through the total giving of the individual and corporate self to become buried. But God, through grace, let some of his people catch a glimpse of this reality, both scripturally and experientially, and the renewal surged forward in unprecedented measure.

The surge seemed to come as the seventies rounded the corner, and it reached great heights by mid-decade. With it came new realities of the presence of God, deepening of commitment, physical and mental healing, and a profound sense of the gathering together of the people of God.

From the earliest days of the renewal there had been a sort of fuzzy awareness that Christians were to "praise the Lord." And they nearly wore the phrase out. After all, the Psalms were filled with such commands as

Let everything that has breath praise the Lord.[1]

And leaders were forever invoking the fact that

. . . thou art holy, O thou that inhabitest the praises of Israel.[2]

We all knew that as we praised him, we somehow enthroned the Lord in our lives. In fact, we were so convinced of this that we enlarged the name of our prayer meetings to "prayer and praise meetings."

But by the turn of the decade, some charismatic leaders, exemplified by Merlin Carothers and Judson Cornwall, were teaching that this praise, which up to then was rather individualistic, coud be lifted to a corporate level in which the living God actually was enthroned in the midst of his church. They and others helped the people to release themselves in worship and adoration of the Father and the Son, through the Spirit.

Moving right along with this, jelling perfectly with

the new dimension in praise, was a steadily growing utilization of music in the worship of God. New music was being brought forth—to stand alongside the more traditional hymns—and was used to enhance and enlarge the periods of worship. The Word of God community in Ann Arbor, Michigan, the Church of the Redeemer in Houston, and others like them—often more liturgy-oriented groups—were in the forefront of this liberating move. In many cases, particularly for newcomers, the music provided a sort of icebreaker into worship. They began by singing their praises and before long they were speaking them, both in their native tongue and in unknown tongues.

With this experience, St. Paul's plea to the church at Rome, discussed earlier, came alive:

Therefore, I urge you, brothers, in view of God's mercy, to offer your bodies as living sacrifices, holy and pleasing to God—*which is your spiritual worship.*[3]

The people found that as they worshiped they gave themselves to God to a degree that had otherwise eluded them. And it worked the other way too: As they gave themselves to God, they worshiped him. At last the light dawned. God did not want anything they might have to offer him by way of sacrifice. He wanted *them.* They came to see that, if they hadn't fully given themselves to God, then they hadn't fully worshiped.

* * * *

The breakthrough on worship touched all aspects of the renewal as people found themselves yielding more to God and becoming increasingly aware of his presence in them and with them. One subtle side effect—and in reality not a side effect at all but rather very central—was that as they yielded to God more completely and more frequently, they found themselves yielding more to one another. They met in Christ. And eventually they opened their eyes and saw one another.

This awareness soon produced a togetherness that exceeded the demands of ministry. They were together to minister as the body of Christ, true, but they were together for something else. It took awhile to penetrate and reach any stage of articulation, but they began to perceive that they were together to hold something in common. And that something was life—the life in Christ, the life of Christ. They were the people of God, and they were to hold in common the things of God.

Teachers began to show that that was the meaning of *fellowship* in the Bible. They began to explain that the word rendered "fellowship" or "communion" in the New Testament is *koinonia* or a related Greek word. It, in turn, means "sharing in common"—denoting the corporate Christian life in which believers share certain realities. It does not mean what we in normal church parlance degraded it to mean—getting together after the service in the fellowship hall to have coffee and tea and talk about the weather or the crab grass. It means holding together our life in God.

In the renewal, our worship together heightened our awareness that the Scripture seemed to call us to share even more together. There were several prominent passages that called us into fellowship. The word "into" was intriguing. It seemed to suggest that as we were being called into Christ—placed in the church by the Spirit—we were being called into something even more advanced, more final, if you will.

One well-studied passage touching on this is in the first letter to the Corinthians. The following verse climaxes a beautiful statement on what we Christians have been given by God in our salvation:

God, who has called you *into fellowship* with his Son Jesus Christ our Lord, is faithful.[4]

God apparently didn't merely save us and grant us eternal life; he has called us into fellowship with Jesus—into the holding of something in common with him. It seems to be a goal, an end, not a means.

Then, that verse can be coupled with another beautiful passage, this one by St. John:

That which was from the beginning, which we have heard, which we have seen with our eyes, which we have looked at and our hands have touched—this we proclaim concerning the Word of life. The life appeared; we have seen it and testify to it, and we proclaim to you the eternal life, which was with the Father and has appeared to us. We proclaim to you what we have seen and heard, *so that you also may have fellowship with us. And our fellowship is with the Father and with his Son, Jesus Christ.*[5]

This passage seems certainly to have been framed to combat rising Gnosticism, establishing that Jesus Christ had indeed come in the flesh and not in some docetic apparition. And its whole expression seems to show that the proclaiming of this true Gospel is for the specific and ultimate purpose of bringing the people into fellowship. And this passage, like the one in First Corinthians, shows us that the fellowship is with Jesus Christ, but it adds the fact that it is also with the Father and, astoundingly, with other believers. All are called into fellowship together—into the holding of life in common. And it does not appear to be a nice little take-it-or-leave-it option. It is the goal toward which everything moves.

Wrapping up the Trinitarian dimension of this fellowship is the great benediction found at the end of St. Paul's second letter to the Corinthians:

> May the grace of the Lord Jesus Christ, and the love of God, and *the fellowship of the Holy Spirit* be with you all.

The fellowship is also with the Holy Spirit. Indeed, because of his function within the Godhead, he is the one who executes the fellowship among God's people on earth—perhaps his ultimate function and the ultimate goal of the charismatic renewal.

* * * *

This awareness of the Bible's call for fellowship did not come without questions and challenges. "How do we work this out?" many asked. "Do you expect us to meet together every day?" others demanded. There did not seem to be clear-cut, once-for-all answers.

The Bible gives us a few verses about the first Christians in Jerusalem, and we studied them, looking for a pattern. They certainly were a community, and a tight one at that. The book of Acts relates:

> They devoted themselves to the apostles' teaching and to the fellowship, to the breaking of bread and to prayer. Everyone was filled with awe, and many wonders and miraculous signs were done by the apostles. All the believers were together and had everything in common. Selling their possessions and goods, they gave to anyone as he had need. Every day they continued to meet together in the temple courts. They broke bread in their

homes and ate together with glad and sincere hearts, praising God and enjoying the favor of all the people. And the Lord added to their number daily those who were being saved.[6]

Further detail is found a few chapters later:

All the believers were one in heart and mind. No one claimed that any of his possessions was his own, but they shared everything they had. With great power the apostles continued to testify to the resurrection of the Lord Jesus, and much grace was with them all. There were no needy persons among them. For from time to time those who owned lands or houses sold them, brought the money from the sales and put it at the apostles' feet, and it was distributed to anyone as he had need.[7]

Apparently, the Christians were together a lot, meeting every day, and they shared everything with one another. And, although it doesn't say so, one senses that many of them must have lived under the same roof. At the very least, it seems, they spent a lot of time under one roof. It is generally thought they came together frequently in various houses, including the home of John Mark's mother, where Jesus may have eaten his last meal with his disciples before his betrayal. That house may even have been the site of the gathering of the Christians on the Day of Pentecost.[8] It does not seem beyond likelihood that many Christians lived there. But those are things we do not know.

We do know, however, from the book of Acts that whatever arrangement they lived under, it did not last. For on the day of Stephen's martyrdom

. . . a great persecution broke out against the church at Jerusalem, and all except the apostles were scattered throughout Judea and Samaria.[9]

For the next several years the details are even skimpier, and the Scripture is relatively silent on the mode of fellowship beyond telling us that in some places church services were conducted in people's homes.

This has led many thoughtful people to question whether the Lord was setting the Jerusalem experience as the model for Christian living. Rather, they suggest, perhaps he was merely showing one possibility and was interested in revealing an *attitude* toward fellowship, preferring to leave the details to be worked out under different circumstances in different locales.

And this was sort of the way things worked out in the current renewal. Many groups of Christians banded together to share households and day-to-day living, the most prominent among them being the Roman Catholic-led communities at Ann Arbor, Michigan, and South Bend, Indiana. But elsewhere there were many variations. In some, the people lived in separate homes, but shared several meals and times of prayer and ministry together each week. Some communities operated with "extended families." Small groups met together for meals, prayer, and sharing anywhere from once to four times a month, but maintained close contact by telephone and irregular meetings in the interim.

In some cases, there was a sharing of homes, food, money, cars, and other major necessities; in others, time, prayer, and Bible study were the main things shared.

The critical point, it seemed, was not the shape of the community, but its attitude, the commitment of individuals first to the Lord and then to one another, the willingness of the individuals to live open lives. Jamie Buckingham, author and pastor, was forever sounding the call—both to the church community in which he lived and pastored in Melbourne, Florida, and to the larger body of Christ—for the living of "transparent lives." He, from the mid-seventies on, exhorted people to get rid of their repressions, to confess their sins, to face themselves and one another squarely, in the Lord.

With different words and a different style, Fullam preached similarly, centering a lot of his teaching on the First Letter of John. Other pastors and teachers found variations on much the same theme.

> This is the message we have heard from him and declare to you: God is light; in him there is no darkness at all. If we claim to have fellowship with him yet walk in the darkness, we lie and do not live by the truth. But if we walk in the light, as he is in the light, we have fellowship with one another, and the blood of Jesus, his Son, purifies us from every sin. If we claim to be without sin, we deceive ourselves and the truth is not in us. If we confess our sins, he is faithful and just and will forgive us our sins and purify us from all unrighteousness.[10]

Of course, "walking in the light" has been a much-taught concept for centuries, with periods of emphasis in pentecostalism and other movements in this century. But the current renewal seemed to bring more determination and a greater breadth than was previously experienced.

"Walking in the light" obviously means walking in a visible manner, openly for all to see—"transparently," in the words of Buckingham. It means clearing out all the little nooks and crannies in which we try to harbor animosities, resentments, grudges, fears, personal sins.

It doesn't necessarily mean sitting around day after day in group confrontations, picking each other apart and badgering each other into repentance, although there were places where such things were done (with questionable results, in my opinion). It doesn't mean spilling every little detail of your life and thought process to everybody who comes along, whether he's interested or whether it's important or not. It doesn't mean giving up your family life, which is ordained by God and would appear to come ahead of community life. It doesn't mean giving up free will or common sense.

It means being nonsecretive—especially in attitude. It means letting the Holy Spirit demonstrate that the bond between you and your fellow Christian warrants the use of the name brother or sister, for it is a stronger bond than flesh and blood ultimately.

Most importantly, one well-known sentence from the above-quoted passage shows that our relationship to God and our relationship to the church depend on our walking in the light:

But *if* we walk in the light, as he is in the light, we have fellowship with one another, and the blood of Jesus, his Son, purifies us from every sin.

The key word is "if." *But if we walk in the light*—then the following good things will happen: We'll have fellowship with one another and our sins will be forgiven. It also says that we should walk in the light

as he is in the light. And we've just read in a preceding
verse that God *is* light; he is all light. James tells us
that God is

The Father of the heavenly lights, who does not
change like shifting shadows.[11]

The King James Version says it familiarly:

. . . the Father of lights, with whom is no
variableness, neither shadow of turning.

Obviously, as we walk in the light, there should be
consistency, no shadows; everything should be visible
for those who want to see—not that everyone will want
to, of course.

Then, and only then, according to John, will the
blood of Jesus cleanse us of our sins. As Fullam was
heard to say so often: "The blood of Jesus does not
cleanse in the dark."

As for the fellowship, experience has proved right
along that for the person not walking in the light—the
one harboring something from or against God or a
brother—fellowship is the last place he really wants to
be. He will gradually but steadily slip away from it. I
know I found that if I was walking in unconfessed sin, I
detested being around people who were free from their
sin through walking in the light.

And confession, according to the First John passage
quoted above, is central to walking in the light:

If we confess our sins, he is faithful and just and
will forgive us our sins and purify us from all
unrighteousness.

Again, the key word is "if." The forgiveness is
conditional. If God does not cleanse in the dark, neither

does he cleanse without confession. Harboring the sin—unconfessed—would be walking in darkness.

Then, John drove home the point regarding fellowship:

Anyone who claims to be in the light but hates his brother is still in the darkness. Whoever loves his brother lives in the light.[12]

Walking in the light is contingent upon a loving relationship with my fellow Christians—with the fellowship. This, with the previous verses, seems to pin the whole Christian life directly on the fellowship. Apparently, I haven't gone very far in my Christian life unless I am in fellowship.

To paraphrase Fullam and other teachers in the renewal: "It would appear that God has made our horizontal relationships with our brothers and sisters the measure—the test—of our vertical relationship with him."

Further, this would appear to apply not only to selected relationships, those with people who appeal particularly to our personalities or life styles. It would apply to all relationships with members of the body of Christ, and especially to those within our spheres of life.

Thus, in the renewal, it has become increasingly clear that the fellowship, the holding of life together, is part of God's great plan for his people, even in the present age. This obviously was the thrust of much of the writing of St. John, reaching beyond the great concerns of St. Paul for the ministry of the body of Christ. John seemed to be reaching for something more profound and more difficult for human beings. Working together, he saw, was going to be easier than living together.

* * * *

The Lord's Sermon on the Mount also provided a nudge toward the fellowship, the unity, of the church. The insight was quite unexpected, at least for me. I was slow to see, for example, that the Beatitudes— which always stunned me with their beauty, their simplicity, and yet their awesomeness—pointed us directly toward relationships with other people, as did the whole sermon, for that matter. Like most Christians, I felt inside myself an unspoken understanding of "the fear of the Lord"—which is a phrase misunderstood by most people—when I dwelt on the Beatitudes. They frightened yet comforted me, depressed yet inspired me, and as my emotions settled I realized I was reverent.

But one day, not too long ago, I comprehended in the sort of "fullness-of-time" way that governs our breakthroughs into new understandings and new opportunities that the Beatitudes would not be realized in a vacuum. They would be realized in the presence of other people—people in our everyday lives, of course, but especially people in the fellowship of believers. They would not be experienced in their fullness by lone-wolf Christians, a category into which I and thousands with personalities like mine tended to slip very easily.

> Blessed are the poor in spirit,
>   for theirs is the kingdom of heaven.
> Blessed are those who mourn,
>   for they will be comforted.
> Blessed are the meek,
>   for they will inherit the earth.

Blessed are those who hunger and
    thirst for righteousness,
  for they will be filled.
Blessed are the merciful,
  for they will be shown mercy.
Blessed are the pure in heart,
  for they will see God.
Blessed are the peacemakers,
  for they will be called sons of God.
Blessed are those who are persecuted
    because of righteousness,
  for theirs is the kingdom of heaven.[13]

It seems clear that those marvelous maxims will be realized—certainly measured and tested—in our relationships with people. "Blessed are the poor in spirit"—*the humble.* Humility is not easily revealed in isolation. The humble will be manifested in the presence of others, as will the meek and the merciful and the peacemakers.

And so it goes through most of the Sermon on the Mount, which St. Augustine regarded as "the perfect measure of the Christian life."[14]

It is certain that as the current renewal progresses, the Christian life will be measured and tested more and more. Especially will this be true as the age speeds up, or slows down, whichever it may be. If, as so many believe, the end of the age is fast rolling in upon us, we can be certain that life will be tested in the extreme.

It is noteworthy that St. Paul touched on this matter of fellowship as he discussed the second coming of the Lord.[15] However, many missed the fellowship remarks as they were dazzled by the words about Christ's return.

First, he discussed those relatively few concrete and unshrouded things we can know about the Lord's coming: The resurrection of the believers is entirely dependent on the resurrection of Jesus; those who have died (fallen asleep) in Christ will rise first, followed by those believers still alive; Christ will apparently remain "in the air" in some manner for some time, calling to himself all the believers, dead and alive; there will be a "loud command," presumably by the Lord, "the voice of the archangel," Michael and Gabriel being the only two we know by name, and finally "the trumpet call of God," the trumpet or the horn having always been the rallying instrument of God; and the believers will be with the Lord forever.

Paul went on to remind the people that, as the Lord himself had said, that day would come "like a thief in the night." There was to be no setting of timetables. The brethren were merely to be "alert and self-controlled,"

> putting on faith and love as a breastplate, and the hope of salvation as a helmet.

And then he made the statement that all Christians need to be reminded of:

> For God did not appoint us to suffer wrath. . . .

The entire passage makes it plain that there may be distress and the kind of suffering that comes merely from trying to live as a Christian in the world. There may be persecution for some, or many. But, he declared flatly, God's people will not suffer God's wrath. Interestingly, in two verses in the passage, he cited the fellowship as the key to grasping these truths and waiting for them to be worked out. In the first, he said:

Therefore encourage each other with these words [about Christ's coming].[16]

And later he added:

Therefore encourage one another and build each other up, just as in fact you are doing.[17]

In other words, he was telling them that while waiting for the fulfillment of these things, while possibly suffering, while watching, they were to be together, building one another up, which is the purpose of the body, as we saw earlier. The instruction is reminiscent of that found in Hebrews:

Let us not give up meeting together, as some are in the habit of doing, but let us encourage one another—and all the more as you see the Day approaching.[18]

The Scripture seems to leave no doubt but that God's people are to be more and more united—although still in the world and ministering to it—as his plan is unfolded. Actually the reason is quite simple. As St. Paul said,

. . .God was pleased to have all his fullness dwell *in him* [Jesus]. . . .[19]

and again,

. . . God has chosen to make known among the Gentiles the glorious riches of this mystery, which is *Christ in you.* . . .[20]

If all the fullness of God dwells in Christ, and if Christ dwells in each Christian, then it is logical that he would much more completely manifest himself in his people when they were together.

The church has—and can manifest—the fullness of God. What would the world think if it saw that fullness?

But the renewal has shown us that serious impediments remain. Can they be overcome?

CHAPTER NINE

The Walls

As we look from this pattern of unity ahead to where the charismatic renewal is heading, we would be helped by understanding what Jesus said about traditions. For many of the things that block unity within the church fall into the category of tradition.

We don't find the Lord criticizing traditions carte blanche. After all, they can be quite neutral. We find him assailing them when they block or inhibit the truth. In fact, the New Testament indicates that Jesus and his followers kept many of the traditions of their fathers. It was only when those traditions misled the people or sealed off the truth that they struck out at them.

The fifteenth chapter of Matthew provides a good illustration. Jesus was challenged for allowing his disciples to break "the tradition of the elders" by not forcing them to undergo the ceremonial washing of hands before eating.

Jesus hit back at that criticism by showing them they were concerned with external rites of cleanliness while speaking and acting in a manner that betrayed internal uncleanliness. He was far more concerned with the heart and what was in it than with a ceremonial washing.

"For out of the heart come evil thoughts, murder, adultery, sexual immorality, theft, false testimony, slander. These are what make a man 'unclean'; but eating with unwashed hands does not make him 'unclean.' "[1]

In other words, the people were being misled into thinking that they stood clean before God merely by washing their bodies, when in fact they needed the Holy Spirit to wash and clean their hearts and minds. A tradition was deceiving the people.

At the end of this exchange with the Pharisees and teachers came a strong statement to his disciples, one that the church near the end of the twentieth century must hear:

. . . Every plant that my heavenly Father has not planted will be pulled up by the roots.[2]

And so it is today. Those traditions, those practices, those structures among God's people that are not of his planting will be torn up. God himself will bring it about.

It seems to me that we can take comfort from this, particularly when we link it with the words of the Lord recorded a bit later by St. Matthew from a talk with Peter and the other disciples about who they thought he was.

. . . I will build my church, and the gates of Hades will not overcome it.[3]

The comfort comes from the certainty of the declarations. God will build the church. God will purify it. It seems that we can stop worrying about it. Of course, we have to be as wise as serpents at all times, but simultaneously we have to be as innocent as doves.[4] All we have to do is follow God. He knows what is of his planting and what is not. We don't always know, at least immediately.

As for traditions in the church today, there would seem to be cases where they are harmless, sort of neutral, but there are also cases where they are clearly harmful. As an Episcopalian who is very fond of that denomination's way of worship for the most part, I am certain that much of what we do is harmful. The blind, thoughtless repetition of prayers and creeds without a searching of the heart and a total yielding of the self to God—which is the practice in many congregations—can serve only to keep the people complacent and closed to the working of the Lord in their lives. Such practices deceive the people and can be expected to anger the Lord. On the other hand, those same prayers and creeds, when uttered by people sincerely giving themselves to the Lord, are known to enhance worship.

The same holds true for traditions and practices in other denominations and among independent bodies, of course. The independent congregation that develops a virtual superstition out of always making a so-called "positive confession" about everything under the sun or of "claiming" this or that from God regardless of whether God is giving it, is just as guilty, it seems to me, of setting up a block to the true working of God. Such mindless tradition is surely no worse than that of some who make the sign of the cross at certain points in their services without fully experiencing the work of the cross internally.

But the comforting truth about all of this is that the

Lord will uproot that which is not from him.

* * * *

As for the building of the church, Christians have for centuries been declaring their belief in "one church" while continuing to live as though there are "many churches." Millions recite creeds to this effect each Sunday. Even those who abhor such fixed worship as the recitation of creeds nonetheless agree with the wording. And yet *we don't live what we say we believe.* It is extremely baffling—even to those on the outside who don't really care.

The Nicene Creed, framed more than 1,600 years ago, says, for example, as noted back in chapter one:

I believe one holy Catholic and Apostolic Church.

And yet there is no evidence anywhere of any such entity. Where is one church that is holy? Where is one church that is catholic or universal, that is apostolic in the sense of faithfulness to the apostles' teaching? And still we say we believe it. As long as we don't deceive ourselves into thinking it has already appeared, the statement of belief is probably good, if we at least move toward it.

In the charismatic renewal, many people left their denominational churches in disappointment over their shortcomings, their hypocrisy in some instances. They pulled out in search of that "one holy Catholic and Apostolic Church," among other things. They often found some of the "other things"—good Bible teaching, or good worship, and sometimes good fellowship. But they never found the one church of the creeds. Some congregations had a lot of things together, but none wholly fit the descriptions found on the pages of the New Testament. In the long run, the Baptists didn't seem to have it all together any better than the

Episcopalians; they merely had different pieces together. The Roman Catholics didn't seem any farther along than the Methodists. The independents were no better ultimately than the Presbyterians. The Pentecostals had as many missing pieces as the Lutherans.

Many people found help and comfort in small home groups, but in the end they seemed to be lacking as much as the others.

The reason was actually a simple one. None of us felt altogether complete merely because we were not altogether complete. Our full experience of completeness will not come until Christ's prayer for "complete unity" is fulfilled.

* * * *

As we reflect on the fact that Jesus is building his church and the additional fact that those parts of it that are not true will ultimately be removed, it enlarges our appreciation to remember just why the church is so important to God. For it is a safe saying that to the Father, the church ranks second in importance only to Jesus Christ.

St. Paul's letter to the Ephesians contains two significant statements about the purpose of the church. In the first, he says:

His intent was that now, *through the church*, the manifold wisdom of God should be made known to the rulers and authorities in the heavenly realms, according to his eternal purpose which he accomplished in Christ Jesus our Lord.[5]

It would seem that some of the wisdom of God has already been revealed to the spiritual world but not all of it. The revelation and its fulfillment is progressive.

But how strange it seems that God would choose the church—the *ekklesia*, the "called-out ones"—through which to make known his wisdom. Strange or not, we can be sure it will be done.

And then a few verses further comes the well-known benediction shedding bright light on the church's significance:

> Now to him who is able to do immeasurably more than all we ask or imagine, according to his power that is at work within us, to him be *glory in the church* and in Christ Jesus throughout all generations, for ever and ever! Amen.[6]

The church is to manifest glory to God through all generations. He gives it its glory and it is given right back to him—an endless cycle. It will be done.

It seems quite logical that a fragmented church, a church failing to manifest the wholeness of God, cannot show forth the wisdom of God or bring glory to him. Only the church that Jesus asked for can do that. And, marvelously, it will at the same time show forth the love of God:

> May they be brought to complete unity to let the world know that you sent me and *have loved them* even as you have loved me.[7]

What does this mean to us? We have been experiencing remarkable renewal, we have experienced the power of God on a scale harking back to the first and second centuries, and yet the church consists of hundreds of divisions, often each going forth without regard to the others. Is this going to continue?

It would seem evident that the Holy Spirit has worked in the renewal in such a way as to reveal a pattern pointing toward unity. Each progression has nudged us in that direction. At this very time, more and more congregations are experiencing the body-of-Christ ministry, and a number are even now moving into deeper fellowship beyond that. The body of Christ is definitely being built up—but in sections. Can the pattern of unity be extended for those sections to be brought together?

* * * *

On the surface, the advice of many in the independent congregations woud seem to be right: The denominations must be broken up if there is to be unity. Large numbers felt this in the early days of the renewal especially. It seemed logical that everyone would be brought out of his denomination and separate group and into the "true body of Christ." Unhappily, as noted earlier, experience has shown that those who "come out" don't have anything better to "go into."

This has led many people to believe God may be doing his work right among the many pieces. The denominations, in their view, may have a longer, more useful life than some expected. God was able to bring unity and strength through diversity in local bodies; perhaps diversity in styles and methods as found in denominations will prove to be no block to unity on a large scale.

Somehow, though, the church must start being seen by the world for what it actually is in God's purpose— one church. With each part still spinning off on its own, how can this be?

Perhaps the Scripture provides a clue for us. In several places it refers to the church at so-and-so—the church of God in Corinth,[8] the church of the Thessalonians,[9] the church in Ephesus,[10] the church in Smyrna,[11] and so on. Today, there are no communities of any substantial size where we can honestly refer to *the* church. It's virtually certain that in all cities the churches look ahead and plan their year or their next five years, or whatever, without consulting one another in any meaningful way. Each acts as though it is the church in that city, but in fact it is not. How can Christians, who are one body in the eyes of God, within the same local area plan to do something without talking about it with the other Christians? But that's the way it's done. It's like one finger on a hand trying to do something without collaborating with the other fingers.

It may be that God's breakthrough on this problem will come at the local level, for such a move is conceivable, at least up to a point, even in the midst of considerable diversity. But it would require a willingness to live out the Beatitudes.

Take Boston, hypothetically. Wouldn't it be possible to maintain, at least for the time being, the individual denominations and independent churches there and yet have them begin to consult regularly and frequently about what they are doing to build up the body of Christ—about a strategy, say? Wouldn't it be possible for the leadership of each to begin sincerely to coordinate plans for outreach, or for the support of missions? Wouldn't it be possible for them to begin to hold the life of Christ in common at least in the area of planning?

They could continue to meet separately, of course, since few cities have facilities large enough to accommodate regular meetings of all the Christians at one time anyhow.

The main thing that could be accomplished under

such an approach would be the development and expression of an *attitude* of oneness in Christ. This would not be easy, for congregations tend to want to do things their way, to clutch their independence tightly to their breasts. To be willing to submit ideas and plans to others for opinions, possible cooperation, and perhaps even criticism would require a great change in attitude.

Never, of course, should any congregation yield on matters of truth, such as those items found in the Apostles' Creed or the Nicene Creed, for example—such foundational truths as the Lordship of Jesus Christ. These matters would have to be agreed upon at the outset. There could be no joining together of believers and nonbelievers.

Beyond these major points of agreement, however, there would be much room for give-and-take if the attitude of love and trust was developed. This would have to be done by the Holy Spirit, of course, and it would be done if there was a willingness on the part of the people to have him do it.

In addition to meeting and sharing in the realm of planning, say, for the year ahead, the congregations could even experiment with meeting together three or four times a year if there was an adequate facility. This would be a time when "the church at Boston" manifested itself to the world. There is no reason to believe that this one step would produce that "complete unity" that Jesus has called for, but it might be progress.

* * * *

The matter of attitude cannot be stressed too much in any consideration of the unity that the Holy Spirit is unmistakably leading God's people into as the century moves toward its close. The Holy Spirit is the Spirit of unity. And if we submit our strong wills to him—if we do our best to maintain an attitude of oneness in the church—he will accomplish that which we cannot.

This is the sort of response God expects from his people—a yielding of the will, of ourselves. Just as in salvation and in the baptism in the Holy Spirit, just as in the experiencing of God's power through the gifts of the Spirit and in all acceptance of God's grace, we must respond at some point to the Lord. That response is a matter of the will, of the attitude.

For example, God is willing to fill us and clothe us with his Spirit, to send us out to minister to the needy all about us, but if we're not interested, if we aren't willing to live in an attitude of acceptance, then nothing happens. God will not violate our wills in these matters. This is not to say that he is not sovereign or that his purpose is ever thwarted, but in one of the mysteries that we are not yet able to fathom, he still desires a response from us.

This is definitely the case with the unity of the church, which may be the ultimate work of the charismatic renewal. If we do not submit our wills to the Holy Spirit and begin to live in an attitude of oneness—even in times when circumstances might not seem to warrant it—then he will not bring us to unity.

But, we can be assured, the Spirit is working within some to arouse a desire to see Jesus' plea fulfilled. He is even at this moment working in desires, nudging, wooing his people toward realization of the goal.

Our part is to come as quickly as possible to that place where we say, "All right, Lord, I yield to you; to the extent possible, I will to be united with my brothers and sisters; I purpose to live in an attitude of complete unity."

Truly the development of this attitude and its implementation must be the ultimate goals of the charismatic renewal. For until we experience genuine fellowship—not only within congregations, but between congregations—we have fallen short of the mark.

This was the attitude of the planners of the great 1978 rally in Giants Stadium, planned and hammered out, often through tears, by leaders drawn from Roman Catholic and Protestant backgrounds. Even if details were not always perfect, they willed and purposed to work in unity. The Holy Spirit took it from there, and the result was a touch of evidence that the church really is one, that Jesus Christ the Lord was sent by the Father, and that God loves his people even as he loved Jesus.

> How good and pleasant it is
>   when brothers live together in
>   unity!
> It is like precious oil poured on the head,
>   running down on the beard,
> running down on Aaron's beard,
>   down upon the collar of his robes.
> It is as if the dew of Hermon
>   were falling on Mount Zion.
> For *there the Lord bestows his blessing*,
>   even life forevermore.[12]

A Postscript

The dictionary says a postscript is "a note or series of notes appended to a completed letter, article or book." I suppose that is what this is.

As I concluded my book on the preceding page, my hand fairly itched to write more, to become more precise, to cut away any fuzziness about where the church's marvelous renewal is heading.

"Perhaps I ought to add a note," I thought.

And then a story occurred to me, and I thought perhaps it would be helpful, maybe encouraging, even though it doesn't offer a lot of exactness. I'm not sure it fully qualifies as a postscript; it certainly is not an epilogue. But if it's a note, it's a pretty long one.[1]

First off, loosen your imagination—sort of close your eyes real tight even though you're faced with the problem of trying to read this—and let it float back 1,950 years or thereabouts to a setting in a rolling, desert-like place. It is midday. Even the air seems softly tan as the dust swirls in the

_____
[1]A version of the following story, written by Bob Slosser, was presented as a monologue over the CBN Radio Network on Pentecost eve, 1970.

noisy wind. We are faced with what really amounts to a wide place in the road, a sort of stopping place for wayfarers.

There is a brownish-gray, clay-sided well. A number of young children are running about, laughing and talking. Three or four quite old people are waiting their turns at the well.

The heat is severe, almost visible. The sunlight is piercing.

A boy, probably sixteen years old, approaches the well. He pulls his gray burnoose back from his forehead, revealing moderately long, wavy, black hair, a tanned face, and a wide smile lighted by extraordinarily white, even teeth.

There is a lot of talk, but the gusting wind plays tricks with it. In the soft, low moan, occasionally rising to a near-howl, his is the only voice we can hear.

Hello. My name is Joash.

May I stop here and rest a moment? My legs are just about ready to fall off.

I certainly would appreciate a cup of water, if it isn't too much trouble.

I left the city this morning and have been walking quite fast most of the time. My sister is sick, and I hope to reach her tonight. She lives out near Jericho.

I didn't want to leave Jerusalem right now, but I felt I had to because of her. She needs help.

This is the most exciting time in Jerusalem I've ever seen. So many marvelous things are happening.

Yes, one thing after another. I'm sure you've heard about them.

Yes, the things about Jesus, the things about the Messiah.

He's my Lord, you know.

Oh, he's really my Lord now—after what happened a week ago. There's no doubt about it. He's the Messiah. He's the King, all right.

Yes, I suppose you haven't heard about this last thing, last week.

Well, it's difficult to explain.

You know, of course, about the killing of Jesus—the crucifixion?

Yes, and about how he rose from the dead and actually appeared to some people? He ate with them and talked with them.

That all happened—and other things too. It went on for about forty days, and then he rose up into heaven right in front of their eyes.

I know. It sounds strange—I know, unbelievable—but it happened. I know those men.

That's right. But I can also tell you personally about some of the things that happened after that, about the miracle last week.

Yes. You see, I happened to be with Jesus quite a few times around Jerusalem. I had never seen anyone like him. I had never felt the way I did when I was with him—when he looked at me.

Yes—and when he touched me.

It was just something new.

I really mean it. It was as though I was another person—I was just changed, that's all. I mean, you know, in my mind and all.

Yes—and, you know, I'm pretty young—I really don't have much. I'm kind of a wanderer, you might say—

Yes, my parents are dead—but those people who had followed Jesus for months and months—and some for years—well, they let me stay with them after he was killed.

That's right—we sort of all stayed together—some of us stayed in one house, and a lot lived around in different places. But we might as well have all lived in the same place—we were together so much.

Yes, I stayed with one of the other young fellows—actually it was his mother's house—a really smart, young guy—John Mark.

This was during those first few days.

And Jesus was still appearing to some.

Yes—he was teaching them—

Yes, all kinds of things—you know, about the Scriptures—how it all tied together—that sort of thing.

No, no, I was never there when that happened.

The really fantastic thing, at least as far as I'm concerned, happened after Jesus had gone—

Yes—right up into heaven.

Well, we all went to this house—John Mark's—where some of us had been staying. We all met there during the day and the evening. Sometimes there'd be as many as a hundred or a hundred and twenty of us jammed in there.

Someone was praying just about all the time—sometimes all of us together—sometimes little groups of three or four. But somebody was praying just about all the time.

And we talked about Jesus almost every minute. Peter—

Yes—Simon, the fisherman—big, old Peter, the one who was so close to Jesus until right there at the end when—well, he was scared, and he ran away—

Well, Peter and John and James—they were close to

the Lord too. They kept telling us about all the things Jesus had taught them, particularly after the resurrection.

That's right—about God and his kingdom—and about forgiveness—

Yes—there was a lot about telling folks about forgiveness—and about new life—

Yes—all this from Jesus—

Yes—a new life with God—that's right.

And there was a lot about Jesus coming again to take us all with him—

That's right, but nobody knew very much about that —nothing very specific.

I know. It sounds strange.

But there was one thing certain during all this. We all knew Jesus was the Son of God, the Messiah. He had given himself for us. He loved us—

Yes—and we knew he was alive and had promised he would be with us always.

We agreed one hundred percent on this.

Yes, that's right—

Oh, sure—we had some differences, but we agreed on this.

And there wasn't one person there who didn't love Jesus with all his heart.

Yes—it's funny about that. Many of us had seen him just a few times and really didn't know much about him—

That's right, but we knew beyond any doubt that he loved us and we loved him—

We really agreed on that—

Anyhow, we stayed together, and prayed and talked and thanked God for all he had given us. We did that practically without stopping for ten days.

Then, just a week ago, on the Day of Pentecost, we were all together, well over a hundred of us, in that upper room, where we had prayed together. Peter was talking to us about the promises Jesus had made, especially about sending the Holy Spirit—the Counselor, he called him.

He told us about how Jesus had said they would be baptized with the Holy Spirit.

Yes—I was puzzled by that.

Me too—I really didn't know what he meant. But he emphasized that Jesus had said they would receive power.

Yes—I wasn't too sure what that meant either.

Oh, boy, that's right—but we were really eager for this just the same—whatever it was. We didn't really know what to expect. We didn't understand. But we knew Jesus had never given us anything that was bad. He had never even spoken a mean word to us, and he apparently was going to give us something he wanted us to have.

That's right. We really wanted it.

And we were praying and praying that day—just sort of saying over and over in a lot of different ways that we wanted his will to be done—sort of like what we had been doing every day.

Then, right there in that room, right there in Jerusalem, not far from the Temple, things began to happen. I mean—I was almost scared. I didn't know what was happening—

Well, there was this sound, like a wind—

Yes—a big, loud wind. It swept right through that room. The door banged—and everything shook. It was really noisy for a second or two—

I know—that's the way I felt. But then we all sat up

162

and looked around. We couldn't see where it was coming from. It was just there.

But then, as this wind sound continued, I wasn't scared any more. The wind was there, but the banging and rattling sort of stopped. I didn't know what was going on, but I knew something good was happening.

Somehow I knew it was good.

And as I looked around, I saw the strangest thing I'd ever seen. But I still wasn't afraid, and I didn't do anything about it. Right there—right in front of my eyes—were these little flames like—these sort of patches of fire—

They were—I don't know—in the air like, and they seemed to be touching everybody there, kind of resting on everyone's head or their shoulders—

No, no—nothing was burning. No, their clothes were okay—and their hair—but those flames were touching them.

And everyone began to talk—

Yes—yes—they all began to talk. They had been really quiet for two or three minutes. It seemed like quite awhile—but then everyone began to talk. They lifted their hands up into the air, and they were looking up, you know, with their heads held back—

Yes, they were just reaching up, like toward heaven. And some were on their knees, and some had fallen flat on the floor, almost like they were unconscious.

But they were all talking—some pretty loud too, and some real soft. They were all talking—to God, to Jesus, you know—like thanking him, and worshiping him, I think.

But do you know what? I noticed in a minute or two that they weren't speaking our language—

That's right. They weren't speaking our language.

In fact, I don't know that they were speaking Greek, or Latin or anything else. I only know that they were speaking in other tongues.

I know myself—I just felt all cleaned out inside—all relaxed and peaceful.

Yes—but at the same time I was excited too—excited and happy. I just felt that, really and truly, all my worries were just washed right out of me. I wasn't afraid any more of being really alone—

That's right. That loneliness—and the fear, you know, that you get with it—well, that was gone. I had Jesus. I really knew it. And I had all those wonderful people. I had them all.

That's exactly right—I had Jesus—and I had him inside me too—all over me—I had him all through me—

That's right— I had him all through my mind, my heart, my legs, my hands, my eyes. I just had the Lord all over—

Yes, I knew all that right then—don't ask me how—and I still know it.

I was actually laughing, chuckling and shaking right down in my stomach—a real deep laugh. And yet tears were running down my cheeks. I could feel them and taste them on my lips.

And my lips—they were moving—real fast—

Yes—yes—and then I realized that I, too, was speaking in an unknown language. I had thought it was just the others, but it was me too.

That's right. And boy what a difference there was as this sound came out of me. I was really free.

That's right—I was really free. All the old stuff that got in my way when I tried to think, or pray, or even talk—all those were gone. I just felt wide open.

Yes—isn't that funny? I was just soaring and singing with this language, or whatever it was—this other tongue.

I really don't know why, or who started us, or exactly how it happened—but as we were all praising God and laughing and singing, really with our spirits, I guess, we began to leave the room.

That's right—we just sort of filed down onto the street, and we weren't very quiet about it either, I'm afraid. We just walked down and headed in the direction of the Temple—

Yes—the Temple—it was there in the square that we just gathered and sort of milled around, praising the Lord and talking—

Yes, there were probably a hundred and twenty of us, all together there—just full of God, that's all—just full of the Lord.

That's right—I know—it must have looked funny, now that I think about it. But I guess that's the way it was supposed to be—because a lot of other people followed us and came and joined in with us—a lot of people from all over the place, people we didn't know. They just milled around with us.

And then we became aware of one other thing—it was strange—but as we praised God in words we really didn't understand these people gathering around us seemed to understand what we were saying. Hundreds of them were gathering around us—thousands, I'd say, at one point.

Yes, that's right—they seemed to understand us. They said we were talking in their languages, you know, in all those foreign languages that those people speak—they said they heard their own languages.

Isn't that something? Imagine—we were talking about God in tongues that we didn't understand, and those people were understanding us in their own languages.

Can you imagine God doing that? He just came right to us—right to all those people there. Isn't that something?

And guess what. A lot of those people thought we were drunk! They said we'd had too much wine—and it was only nine o'clock.

I'll tell you—I didn't need any wine—that's for sure—that was far better than wine—

Yes—don't you see? We were filled with the Holy Spirit—just covered with him—just what Jesus had promised. He had said we'd be baptized with the Holy Spirit, and we had been. It was really something—

Yes, that's right. It sure caused quite a stir. In fact, it got so rowdy that Peter finally stood up on some steps and started to speak to the people—I bet there were five thousand of them jammed in there by that time— maybe more. Of course, they couldn't all hear him, but he talked real loud, and quite a few of them could understand what he was saying.

Yes—I'll never forget the way he explained it—it was great. He just told them about the Scriptures, and about the prophet Joel, and some other things, and it all made sense. It was just really good—

Yes—he can sure speak out when he wants to—and I've never heard him do it better.

In the last days, God says,
    I will pour out my Spirit on all people.

That's the way he said it—just like that—in that big, deep voice he has. And he told them all about what Joel had said—

Yes, that's right—he really seemed to understand that very well—he just knew it.

And the thing that he really drove home was the part

about everyone who calls on the name of the Lord will be saved. He really made that clear.

And big, old Peter—he's really something—and I'd never heard him talk like that before—so big and strong—and so tender at the same time.

He just told them all about Jesus and how he was crucified and killed, and how God let it happen. And he told how he was buried and all that—and then how he was resurrected—raised up right before their eyes—and how he was taken right up to the right hand of the Father—exalted, he said—

Yes, that's right. He said Jesus was taken up to the right hand of God, where he received the promise of the Holy Spirit for his people and had poured him out—that's what he said—he poured him out right there that day.

Isn't that something? The Holy Spirit was poured out on the disciples of Jesus right there in Jerusalem.

But Peter made a big point out of this—he said it wasn't just for us right there, right then.

No—that was important—he said something about the gift—that's what he called the Holy Spirit—the gift was for them and also for all the others who would follow him later on—their children, and their children's children—that's what Peter said.

He said they just had to understand that Jesus was the Lord, the Messiah—

Yes—Lord and Messiah—

Yes—Jesus—the one who would forgive their sins.

That's right. It was really something that day. I know it's pretty hard to believe, but I found out later that some three thousand people were baptized that day—just in that one day. Can you believe it? Three thousand. I don't see how we ever baptized that many—it just never seemed to stop.

I actually heard little children—and their parents—and some people who were just real old—all of them—just giving themselves to Jesus right there—

Yes—I watched them. They were crying and laughing and talking, all at once. It's really something to hear a little child talking right to the Lord.

It was strange. He was right there—as strange as it sounds—he was right there. They couldn't see him with their eyes—but he was there. He touched them—and they touched him—in a way.

I know. Yes—it's hard to explain. I know—but that's the way it was. I was there. I saw it.

Oh, no—no—quite the opposite. It's continued. It hasn't gone—it wasn't like a dream—like waking up from a dream—

No. Not at all. Jesus is here. He's real. He's the Lord—the real Lord.

Oh, that—no. That stayed too. It's funny—I didn't really think it would.

Yes. The next day—I was just talking to the Lord, and thanking him, you know, for that wonderful time—and you know—I just wanted—it was more than that—I really deep down wanted to talk to him the way I had the day before—you know, just between him and me—just loving him, and telling him—

That's right. I wanted to speak in that unknown language. And do you know what?

That's right—I did.

Yes—the same way. He hadn't taken it away. I could just turn myself loose right into his arms. It was really something.

Yes—that's right—yes—but something else really struck me then and in the days ahead. It became more and more obvious to me—and to the others too. As I gave myself to the Lord in a way that I never had before—I mean, I didn't want to hold anything back— well, as I did that I found myself feeling closer and closer to old Peter and John and the others—all of them.

Yes—can you see it? As I was more and more aware of God, I was more and more aware of the others. After all, he was in them too.

I soon found that the others were feeling the same way. We wanted to be together—and I have a hunch that the time will come when we will need to be together. We give each other strength. And we sort of fit together, somehow, in a way that we can get things done better. We just sort of go together—I don't know—like one strong person, maybe.

We're planning to stay very close together in the future. A lot of us will be living together and sharing meals together—and of course we'll be praying together like always—seeking the Lord's will.

Yes—you see—he told us we'd be going around taking the news about his kingdom everywhere—

Yes—about the Father's love and forgiveness—

Yes—but most of us really don't see how we're going to do that.

Yes, we sure will—we will really need one another.

Yes. I know it sounds strange. It's still a little strange to me—a mystery like.

But that's the way it is.

Well, I've been holding you folks up far too long. I know you've got things to do.

Yes, and I've got to get going myself. It's still quite a way, and I want to get there in time to pray for my sister tonight.

Yes—yes—you see, I'd like to get back for the

meeting tomorrow night. They'll all be there.

Yes—I know—I'm going to have to hurry. But it's funny—as young as I am, they still need me. That's what they say anyhow. I know I sure need them.

Thanks for the water and the chance to rest. I sure enjoyed visiting with you.

Yes—yes—that's right. It's all going to work out. Praise God.

Notes

Chapter One
[1]John 17:23.
[2]John 3:16.
[3]The Nicene Creed and Apostles' Creed.

Chapter Two
[1]John 3:1-21.
[2]John 3:7-8.
[3]Genesis 1:1.
[4]Genesis 1:2.
[5]Genesis 1:26.
[6]1 Corinthians 12:4-6.
[7]Ezekiel 36:24-27.
[8]Ezekiel 37:14.
[9]Matthew 28:19.
[10]2 Corinthians 3:6 and Nicene Creed.
[11]2 Corinthians 3:16-18.
[12]John 5:19.
[13]John 16:13-15.
[14]John 6:44.
[15]1 Corinthians 2:4-5.

Chapter Three
[1]Hebrews 3:7-4:7.
[2]2 Corinthians 6:11-13.
[3]Genesis 12:1-4.
[4]Genesis 17:1-2.
[5]Genesis 17:3-5.
[6]Genesis 17:6-8.

[7]Galatians 3:7-9.
[8]Genesis 17:9-12.
[9]Deuteronomy 10:12-13.
[10]Deuteronomy 10:14.
[11]Deuteronomy 10:15.
[12]Deuteronomy 30:19-20.
[13]Deuteronomy 10:16.
[14]Deuteronomy 30:6.
[15]Jeremiah 9:25-26.
[16]Acts 7:51.
[17]Romans 2:28-29.
[18]Galatians 4:6.
[19]Romans 8:14-16.
[20]Matthew 11:30.
[21]Luke 11:11-13.
[22]Luke 11:9.
[23]Revelation 3:20.

Chapter Four

[1]John 14:12, Revised Standard Version.
[2]New International Version.
[3]Luke 4:14-15.
[4]Luke 4:16.
[5]Luke 4:16-19.
[6]Luke 4:20-21.
[7]Luke 3:22.
[8]Luke 7:22-23.
[9]John 20:22.
[10]Luke 24:45-48.
[11]Luke 24:49.
[12]Acts 1:3-5.
[13]Acts 1:8.
[14]1 Corinthians 12:13.
[15]Acts 8:14-19.
[16]Acts 10:44-46.
[17]Acts 1:6-8.
[18]Acts 1:6.
[19]Acts 1:7-8.
[20]Acts 2:1ff.
[21]Acts 2:22-23.
[22]Acts 2:23.
[23]Acts 2:24.
[24]Acts 2:32.
[25]Acts 2:33.
[26]Acts 2:36.
[27]Psalm 124.

Notes

Chapter Five

[1]Exodus 3:10.
[2]Exodus 3:11.
[3]Exodus 4:10.
[4]Exodus 4:11-12.
[5]Exodus 4:13.
[6]Exodus 4:14.
[7]Jeremiah 1:6.
[8]Acts 2:38-39.
[9]1 Corinthians 12:7.
[10]1 Corinthians 12:11.
[11]1 Corinthians 12:4-6.
[12]Ephesians 2:10.
[13]1 Corinthians 14:1.
[14]1 Corinthians 12:8-11.
[15]1 Corinthians 14:5b.
[16]1 Corinthians 14:2,4.
[17]1 Corinthians 14:28.
[18]Jeremiah 23:16.
[19]Jeremiah 23:18.
[20]Jeremiah 23:22.
[21]1 Corinthians 14:3.

Chapter Six

[1]1 Corinthians 15:50-52.
[2]John 3:16.
[3]Philippians 2:5-8.
[4]Ephesians 2:10.
[5]John 1:12-13 & John 3:3.
[6]Romans 12:1-2.
[7]Matthew 11:28-30.
[8]Matthew 25:14-30.
[9]Numbers 11:16-17.
[10]Exodus 35:30-36:1.
[11]Judges 14:19.
[12]Luke 3:21.
[13]Luke 4:1.
[14]Luke 4:14.

Chapter Seven

[1]1 Corinthians 12:12.
[2]1 Corinthians 12:27.
[3]1 Corinthians 12:13.
[4]Ephesians 4:3-4.
[5]Colossians 1:18.
[6]Ephesians 1:22-23.
[7]Ephesians 5:23.

[8]1 Corinthians 2:9-16.
[9]Acts 15:28.
[10]Acts 13:1-3.
[11]1 Corinthians 12:18.
[12]1 Corinthians 12:14-27.
[13]1 Corinthians 12:22-25.
[14]Mark 10:42-44.
[15]Galatians 3:26-28.
[16]1 Corinthians 14:40.
[17]Ephesians 4:7-16.
[18]Acts 6:2-4.
[19]Acts 2:42.
[20]Acts 20:28-31.
[21]1 Peter 5:1-3.
[22]Ephesians 5:21.
[23]Titus 1:6-9.
[24]Ezekiel 34:25.
[25]1 Timothy 2:7.
[26]2 Timothy 2:15.
[27]2 Timothy 2:23-25.
[28]2 Timothy 3:16.
[29]2 Timothy 2:2.
[30]Malachi 2:7.

Chapter Eight
[1]Psalm 150:6.
[2]Psalm 22:3, King James Version.
[3]Romans 12:1.
[4]1 Corinthians 1:9.
[5]1 John 1:1-3.
[6]Acts 2:42-47.
[7]Acts 4:32-35.
[8]*Early Christian Worship*, Cullman.
[9]Acts 8:1.
[10]1 John 1:5-9.
[11]James 1:17.
[12]1 John 2:9-10.
[13]Matthew 5:3-10.
[14]*The Preaching of St. Augustine.*
[15]1 Thessalonians 4:13-5:11.
[16]1 Thessalonians 4:18.
[17]1 Thessalonians 5:11.
[18]Hebrews 10:25.
[19]Colossians 1:19.
[20]Colossians 1:27.

Chapter Nine
[1]Matthew 15:19-20.

Notes

[2]Matthew 15:13.
[3]Matthew 16:18.
[4]Matthew 10:16.
[5]Ephesians 3:10-11.
[6]Ephesians 3:20-21.
[7]John 17:23.
[8]1 Corinthians 1:2.
[9]1 Thessalonians 1:1.
[10]Revelation 2:1.
[11]Revelation 2:8.
[12]Psalm 133.

SUGGESTED READING

MIRACLE IN DARIEN by Bob Slosser
Agreeing together, a rector and his people set out to try an experiment in faith. determined to conscientiously follow the guidelines of God's Word, they allowed Christ to become the true head of their church. Bob Slosser reports the miraculous results.
P427-5 $4.95

THE HOLY SPIRIT AND YOU by Dennis and Rita Bennett
An easy-to-understand, comprehensive teaching on the person and work of the Holy Spirit. One of the classics on the subject, with over 350,000 books in print. Also features a study supplement for individual or group use.
L324-4 $3.95
Supplement P031-5 $2.95

THE HOLY SPIRIT AND POWER
paraphrased by Clare Weakley
Stunning paraphrase of John Wesley's preaching yields important understanding of the work of the Holy Spirit in the life of the believer. Includes teachings on devotion, repentance, holiness, and the fruit and gifts of the Holy Spirit.
P262-6 $3.50

Available wherever Logos books are sold
Write for information to: Logos International Book Catalog Dept.
Plainfield, NJ 07060 USA

Read the influential magazine of today's worldwide spiritual renewal—**Logos Journal**

Sold in many Christian bookstores
Write for information to:
Logos Journal
201 Church St., Plainfield, NJ 07060 USA